Struggle for FREEDOM

by Knofel Staton

You can obtain a 40-page leader's guide to accompany this paperback. Order number 1965 from Standard Publishing or your local supplier.

A Division of Standard Publishing
Cincinnati, Ohio 45231
No. 40034

© 1977, The STANDARD PUBLISHING Company
a division of Standex International Corp.

Chapter themes based on International Bible Lessons for Christian Teaching, © 1973 by the Lesson Committee.

Library of Congress Catalog Card No. 76-18381
ISBN 0-87239-063-2

Printed in U.S.A. 1977

Table of Contents

Preface 7
1 An Enslaved People 9
2 A Leader Called 18
3 Let My People Go 27
4 Celebration of Freedom 35
5 Commitment to a Covenant 40
6 The Necessity of Worship 45
7 Living It Out 51
8 Light in the Darkness 58
9 Empty Revival 63
10 The Unchanging Message 68
11 Gideon: God's Courageous Man 75
12 Strength Out of Control 81
13 The Use or Abuse of Liberty 87

PREFACE

Freedom! What a universal concern! Nations go to war to get or to keep it. Children run away from home in search of their idea of it. Married couples divorce to have their definition of it. Indebted people declare bankruptcy to get out of responsibility—one idea of freedom. Some move to the city in search of anonymity—another idea of freedom. Others move to the country in search of fewer pressures and more flexible schedules—another concept of freedom. Sociologists speak about freedom from others—environment. Psychologists speak about freedom from self.

But what is freedom? How is it obtained? What are the responsibilities that go along with it? What is the role of others in my freedom—such as parents in the home and leaders in the group or nation? What is the role of God in man's quest for freedom?

The desire and struggle for freedom is not new. It is as old as the Garden of Eden, where Adam and Eve rebelled against God. That rebellion brought enslavement rather than freedom. From that experience we learn that real freedom from slavery is connected to our relationship to God, the Creator and Lord of all the universes—and the liberator of all.

The Israelites' struggle for freedom turns the spotlight upon this God-man encounter and its relationship to freedom.

There are many lessons to learn from this history. One is that when we put freedom, for freedom's sake, in the center of the spotlight, God is too often not clearly seen.

Real freedom is hidden. But when we put God in the center of the spotlight, real freedom results—whether or not we were intentionally seeking it. And there is a good reason, for as freedom is a universal concern, God is the universal One. Only He can meet the universal needs of humanity. Faith in Him frees us from fetters—whatever they may be.

Knofel Staton
Joplin, Mo.

1

An Enslaved People

Exodus 1, 2

They had been a free and a blessed people; but now, from all external manifestations, they looked like a fettered and cursed people. Since the Egyptian king's program had been in force many years, I suppose it would have been easy for editorials of the local paper to speak of the "inferior race among us." Prejudices against the Israelites were widespread. They were a people considered to be good for physical labor only. The people who had previously specialized in caring for animals (Genesis 47:1) were now being treated as animals.

Why? Because of prejudice that resulted in discrimination (mistreatment). It is possible to harbor prejudice without unfair treatment being the result. It is also possible to make distinctions without having prejudice, but quite often the two go hand in hand. Whenever prejudices cause discrimination, discrimination will in turn feed and nurture the continuation and spread of the prejudices. Thus in Exodus 1 we find the people of God being treated unfairly and with differentiation.

A people in the majority became a minority group. Minority groups are of two kinds: those that are few in number and those that are lower in status. Although the descendants of Abraham were numerically in the majority (Exodus 1:9), they were being treated as a minority group (low status). A student of minority groups defines them as having "exclusion from full participation of life in society caused by the exploitation of a dominant group who functions with a higher social status and privilege." One segment of society in Egypt was taking advantage of the descendants of Jacob, another segment of society.

Although it is never God's will that any group of people be put down by another group, God can and does bring His good out of our evils. It has rightly been said that man's extremity is God's opportunity. From the enslavement of these people, God acted to demonstrate His eternal redemptive plan for all humanity. Every man has his "Egypt" (sin) and his "Pharaoh" (Satan). But God will provide a Savior like Moses (Deuteronomy 18:18; Acts 3:22). The events that later occurred during the Israelites' escape from Egypt parallel all people's exodus from sin (the death of a firstborn son—Jesus; forsaking the former life—repentance; crossing the sea—baptism; receiving the law—the new law; Passover—Lord's Supper; the Passover lamb—Jesus).

Growth in Slavery

The king thought he could slow down the numerical growth of the Israelite community by working them to death, but it did not work (Exodus 1:12-14). Their slavery increased in two ways: in number and in the level of their enslavement. The more they grew in number, the more deeply they became enslaved.

Slavery was not just restricted to that time in history; even today many of us are slaves and become more enslaved each day. The more we progress in this way, the tighter becomes our enslaved status.

We can become enslaved to work. In his book, *Confessions of a Workaholic,* Wayne Oates claims that our culture has programmed us to become addicted to work. We are constantly in competition with others concerning the amount of work we do. We can't say "no" to people who desire our services. We feel guilty if we aren't going, going, going constantly. We pride ourselves and say, "We would rather burn out for Jesus than rust out." We can't find the time to take a "day off," even though God did. We don't know how to relax. We don't have time to spend with our children doing "their" things. We are always thinking of the next task that confronts us. The tragedy is that the more we get done, the more we get hooked on work, the more remains to be done, and the less free we are to be balanced people of God.

Howard Hendricks tells how he solves this tendency to become enslaved to work. He writes in his date book on certain days the word "nothing." When someone calls and asks, "What are you doing on the weekend of January 15?" he looks at his book and sees "nothing" written in and replies, "Nothing." Immediately the caller is joyful and asks him to be their group's featured speaker. To that Dr. Hendricks replies, "You misunderstood me; I said I was doing *nothing* that weekend."

Is it possible that Christian leaders are making workaholics out of God's people today? Do we make Christians feel guilty if they do not show up every time the church door is open? Do the preachers allow the members to know the joy of rest and retreat? And do the church members allow the preacher that necessity? Perhaps we need a "Moses" with the courage to say in the face of the workaholic slavery, "Let my people go."

Another type of slavery is the opposite of the workaholic. Coining a new word, I would call it the slavery of the *dependaholic*. The dependaholic does not work but depends on handout programs to keep him going. At this very time I am writing, the unemployment rate is the highest in our country in nearly forty years. Yet last week, a strawberry farmer in Illinois could not find enough people who would work (the unemployed were all around him), so he volunteered to give away his strawberry crop to the nuns of a nearby hospital if they would pick it.

As the benefits multiply, some people become more deeply involved in the dependaholic slavery. Isn't it time that a "Christian nation" heed Paul's advice, "if anyone will not work, neither let him eat" (2 Thessalonians 3:10)?

It is possible that there are some people who could be called dependaholics in our churches. The New Testament teaches that each Christian is to use his life to build up other Christians (1 Corinthians 12; Ephesians 4), but some in the church have buried their talents and draw benefit from the talents of others. They become easily enslaved to the idea, "I have nothing to offer the church."

In this land of wealth and plenty, it is easy to become slaves to possessions. As people acquire possessions, they become proud. What they have is never satisfying for very long, so they seek to accumulate more. There is no end to the list of things they want and "need." It is not long before their goals, thoughts, and activities center around their quest for possessions. Their moral and spiritual values slowly take second place to the lust for money and what it can buy. They no longer relate well to others; they relate only to things and use people to further their quest for possessions. Those enslaved in this way seldom realize how trapped they are. They wonder why they are miserable and lonely amidst their riches and luxuries.

Some people can become enslaved to new ideas; they begin to feel that nothing is worthwhile unless it is new or creative. The exact opposite is the slavery to traditions. Although many traditions are good, we get into a rut when we feel we can only do what has been done before.

Some people get hooked on being accepted by others at any cost. This type of slavery results in all kinds of "rigorous labor." Honesty gives way to dishonesty; purity gives way to ulterior motives; individuality gives way to being molded by others' expectations. This enslavement keeps a person from sharing his problems with someone who could help because "I don't want anyone to know." The more one deceives others in order to be accepted, the more he becomes enslaved to deception.

Some people are enslaved to independence. "We have pulled ourselves up by our own bootstraps and need no one else." Their motto is, "When the going gets tough, the tough get going." This attitude contradicts the New Testament concept of fellowship, which includes members needing each other.

Yes, our "Pharaohs" are many, but these enslavements that have been mentioned are not restricted to individuals only. A family, a country, a congregation, or a brotherhood of congregations can slip into any of the above forms of slavery. It is possible that an entire congregation could be termed *workaholic.* The church calendar is filled every day of the week, and the word "rest" is anathema. A congregation could also be termed *dependaholic;* she is never mature enough to carry her own load. She always depends upon the area men's fellowship to pay the preacher or upon other churches to support the local camp, Bible college, or missions projects.

A church can become enslaved to possessions; she adds buildings and beautiful fixtures and becomes enslaved to the budget needed to pay for it all. The building becomes more important than the people who are to fill and use it.

A congregation can become enslaved to new ideas, building a program on creative gimmicks to get attention and big crowds, forgetting the importance of the "old"

13

gospel message. It is even easier for a church to become enslaved to traditions. Much progress is stopped by the phrase, "We've never done it that way."

Many a congregation is a slave to the acceptance of others. Her attitudes and actions are determined by what is the "in" thing in the community. In one location where I ministered, I wrote a letter to the local newspaper protesting the striptease shows at the county carnival. I received more protest from the church members than from anyone else. They wanted the church to be acceptable in the community and were afraid I was stirring things up too much.

Such slavery is even taught in our churches. I once heard a leader of a congregation teach a Sunday-school class on Luke 11:5-8 *(King James Version).* He pronounced the word "importunity" as "importanty" and proceeded to explain that the man gave in to his neighbor because of the important position the neighbor held in the community. He then made the application that the church should do whatever the important people in the community want it to do.

And how easy it is for a congregation to be enslaved to the goal of functioning independently from others! "Their program and problems are theirs and ours are ours!" We do not take much time for cooperation and communication between congregations. If we are of the New Testament, we have an obligation to cooperate with one another.

The Hebrews moved out of the Egyptian slavery. But eventually they entered into each of these other kinds of slavery we have been considering. They became enslaved to their rituals, to their possessions, to new ideas, to their traditions, to their desire to be accepted by their neighbors, to immorality, and to independence. By the time Jesus came, some groups within Judaism were acting as independent from other groups within Judaism, as some denominations do today.

We must never forget that the freedom that really frees is never the right to do what we please, but to please to do what is right. The former enslaves us to desire; the latter liberates us as humans who can function for God and for others.

Each type of slavery we have today shares at least one common factor with the slavery of the Hebrews in Egypt—the exclusion from full participation in society. To become enslaved to any one of these aspects hinders the other important aspects from properly functioning in our lives. We need what the Hebrews needed—deliverance, so that a balanced people and a balanced nation can result.

Deliverance

But how does deliverance from the seeming hopelessness of slavery come? God must intervene to change the situation. To do so, God uses a human as His instrument. In Egypt, He used Moses; in your Egypt, He may use you.

It takes courage to become a leader who will stand against the oppressor of an enslaved people—regardless of who the oppressor is. Moses saw what was going on around him, and he recognized the oppressor (Exodus 2:11). For being sensitive to what was happening around him, he is to be commended. But for his resulting act of violence, he is not (2:12). Even the oppressed people knew that a man bent on making changes by violence could not be trusted (2:14).

The initial greatness of Moses is seen in the status of his life when he saw the conditions around him. He was a part of the establishment that had initiated and was maintaining oppression. Although he was nursed by his own Hebrew mother for around three years (2:7-9), he grew up as the Pharaoh's grandson (2:10) and was educated as an Egyptian. But he did not cater to the establishment; he had high moral ethics. He chose the uncomfortable position of identifying himself with the enslaved rather than

15

with the seemingly secure position of the masters. He did not rationalize the prejudices that filled his education.

In that perspective, he stood on God's side, for God is concerned for the oppressed regardless of who they may be. God wanted the Hebrew people to be concerned and to be a blessing to all the nations (Genesis 12:2-4). If any people should henceforth be sensitive to the oppressed, it should be these Hebrew people. But the irony of ironies is that they eventually arose to oppress others. (One of God's disappointments in them was that they did not manifest a deliverer's attitude toward the exploited. See Isaiah 1:17; Amos 5:21-24.)

God later sent another deliverer, His Son, to die for humanity and to demonstrate what it means to live for humanity. Jesus took the side of oppressed people. He looked with compassion and care upon those who were being put down in His day (women, children, sick, poor, Gentiles, Samaritans, etc.). In fact, He made it clear that He stood with the minority groups of His day:

> The Spirit of the Lord is upon Me, because He anointed Me to preach the gospel to the poor. He has sent Me to proclaim release to the captives, and recovery of sight to the blind, to set free those who are downtrodden, to proclaim the favorable year of the Lord.
> —Luke 4:18, 19

When Jesus declared, "Today this Scripture has been fulfilled in your hearing" (Luke 4:21), the people in His hometown synagogue rejoiced. But when He explained that it meant He would take a position against their racial prejudice, they tried to kill Him (Luke 4:25-29).

Studying about God helping the enslaved Hebrews can be a nice non-disturbing lesson of history in our Sunday schools. But the lesson is not taught until this disturbing truth comes breaking into our lives: God hates it when people manipulate, use, exploit, and put down other people.

Yes, there are many different kinds of slavery and oppressors, but the worst oppressors are those who think they are better than someone else and act like it. This is the same arrogance and pride that belonged to the Pharaoh of Egypt (Exodus 9:17). No person has any more right to exist than any other, and no one has the right to prosper at the expense of another.

Freedom

God's people are not to live as lords over others, but rather as slaves for them (Matthew 20:25-28). One of the functions of the Spirit of Christ is to set us free for one another (not from one another) so we can serve each other in love (Galatians 5:1, 13).

Jesus as God's second Moses came to deliver all of mankind from the shackles of both human and supra-human "gods." This was prophesied long before He came:

Make ready the way of the Lord, make His paths straight. Every ravine shall be filled up, and every mountain and hill shall be brought low; and the crooked shall become straight, and the rough roads smooth; and all flesh shall see the salvation (deliverance) of God.
—Luke 3:4-6; Isaiah 40:3-5.

So may not only the Hebrews know that God frees from slavery, but may all people see this truth as they watch us take off our fetters and be used by God to help take off theirs. Only then can a diverse people get on the road to becoming a united community.

2

A Leader Called

Exodus 3, 4

"Does Jesus care? ... Oh yes, He cares; I know He cares ..." That's the way the song goes, but is that the way Jesus is? Does He really care about our situations, particularly whenever we are shackled by one kind of slavery or another? There are many oppressed people in the world under many different kinds of oppression, both physical and spiritual. Some have been oppressed people for generations. Is there any compassion from God?

Oh, yes, God cares, although the passing of time may cause us to be insensitive to His care. It is easy to know about generations of some oppressed people and conclude that that is just the way it is and that it must surely meet with God's approval. But God sees the circumstances of the oppressed and hears their cries

(Exodus 3:7, 9), even though they have been oppressed a long, long time (Exodus 12:40). To help the oppressed, God needs individuals who will take God's perspective and dare to share it with the national leaders of the day. It is not an easy task but an essential one.

Moses had turned his back on caring for millions of oppressed people. Instead, he turned to caring for some animals. He had settled down to a peaceful life with his family and job. The Hebrews would have to squirm out of their situation without him! After all, he had tried to help them once, and they did not appreciate it. He probably felt that at least the animals seemed grateful for his efforts for them.

It was easy to be content in the land of Midian. There was no stately palace like that of Pharaoh, but the tent was warm and dry. There was no glittering court, but there was a happy and loving family. Luxuries were few, but food and clothing were plentiful. The life of a desert shepherd was not easy, but it was free from the pressures and tricky intrigues of the capital city. There were no idle rich living for pleasure, but neither were there any overworked and beaten slaves. Moses lived in Midian for forty years, and it seems that he was quite willing to stay there the rest of his days.

But Cain's question had to be asked: "Am I my brother's keeper?" God's answer to that question is yes! God called Moses to a service of leading a whole mass of people out of their oppression. This was a very physical ministry—leading people out of an environment—but it was to have significant spiritual ramifications for all time.

While it is true that our spiritual situation can affect our physical surroundings, it is also true that our physical surroundings can sometimes affect our spiritual situation. I am not suggesting that we should always change our environment in order to heighten our relationship with God; for even though the Hebrews came out of slavery, they later regressed into idolatry and immorality. I am suggesting that sometimes taking the person out of the slum can help him become more open to allowing the slum to be taken out of him. It is a cop-out to proudly announce, "The church is never to be interested in taking the people out of a bad environment, but only in taking the bad environment out of the people." God called Moses to lead the people of Israel out of their bad, oppressing environment, so they could serve God (Exodus 4:23).

Moses, the Leader

According to today's view of leadership qualities, Moses would have been an unlikely candidate for the job God had in mind. He was a murderer (Exodus 2:12) and a fugitive (2:15). He had already been rejected by the very people God wanted him to help (2:14). The first one-third of his life had been spent as a part of the establishment (the oppressors), and the second one-third was spent as a runaway. What did he know about the thinking of the Hebrews? He had been too detached from them to become their leader. It is little wonder that he asked, "Who am I that I should do this?" (3:11).

Neither did Moses have the gift of persuasive speech (Exodus 4:10). He was an unknown who did not communicate well. He was married to a woman of another country (2:21), and already an old man (7:7). He evidently had not been following closely the religious requirements of the Hebrews, for his son was not circumcised (4:24, 25).

Somehow we have overlooked the qualifications for leadership that God desires in people and have substituted our own. A pulpit committee of a congregation of one hundred members would no doubt reject any "Moses" who sought to be a leader in their church. What church would want a preacher who tried to set himself up as a leader, murdered, ran away from the law, went abroad to tend sheep for forty years, and then came back with a message that he had difficulty communicating?

But we mustn't blame the pulpit committee too much. What about yourself? Have you already rejected yourself as a tool in the hands of God? Have you compared yourself with other leaders and said, "I don't have what it takes?" Paul said, "When they measure themselves by themselves, and compare themselves with themselves, they are without understanding" (2 Corinthians 10:12).

Just what is necessary to be used by God? You must see a need, know that God is concerned about it, recognize your inadequacies, believe that God will help you, and commit yourself so that God can work through you. Moses fulfilled these qualifications. He knew the need of the Hebrew people, and he cared about that need. He knew that God cared (Exodus 3:7). He certainly knew his personal inadequacies (3:11, 13; 4:1, 10, 12, 13). But in the face of his weaknesses, he came to grips with God's strengths (3:12, 14; 4:2-9, 11-13) and committed himself to be used by God (4:18-31).

Moses' excuses were legitimate concerns. Certainly we can identify with them. Haven't you ever backed off from a responsibility because of personal inadequacies that seemed to you to make the task impossible to accomplish? Why don't we instead look for strengths that we can use to fulfill responsibilities? Don't we tend to enlist leaders only on their strengths? It may be that we have overlooked some great potential leaders.

We can learn from Moses (and from Paul) that the greatest leaders are those who recognize their weaknesses and lean upon God's strengths. They do not easily get caught in the trap of pride because their weaknesses keep them humble. Paul learned the truth of God: "My grace is sufficient for you, for power is perfected in weakness" (2 Corinthians 12:9). God has often called people who do not fit the Madison Avenue image of leadership, so they will boast in God and not in themselves (1 Corinthians 1:26-31).

Christianity need not try to copy the success of big business executives to build "big churches." That is not our goal. Our goal is to help lead people out of the evil situations of men into lives of service and worship of God. We must quit reading books on how to make a million dollars or how to succeed in big business in order to copy the principles therein for leadership and success.

Some ministers are suggesting this is the way for churches to succeed in our society. But Jesus made it clear that God's leaders were not to be cut out of the same pattern as the secular leaders (Matthew 20:25, 26). From considering the failure of Pharaoh and the success of Moses, it should be clear which kind of leadership lasts. The Pharaoh depended upon self-strength; Moses depended upon God.

Moses' Task

"But the task of helping broken humanity or an erring nation is too big for little ole' me," you say. Look at Moses' task. He was to go to the Pharaoh and demand the release of the people. Can you picture it? There were perhaps three million Hebrews laboring for little or nothing. Would the Pharaoh give that up? The task God gave Moses was like asking you to go to Moscow on a TWA flight tomorrow morning and demand that all the prisoners be released out of the salt mines. No wonder Moses balked. If God gave us such an order, we would probably ask for His driver's license to check His identification. Moses faced a tough assignment.

And once you made it to the salt mines in Russia, how would you know if the people would follow you to freedom or not? Especially if their lives were in the balance. They would ask, "Well, who are you, anyway?" It is not surprising that God gave miraculous powers to Moses to authenticate his person and message. God gave miraculous signs to Moses in response to his question, "What if they will not believe me, or listen to what I say?

22

For they may say, 'The Lord has not appeared to you' "
(Exodus 4:1). God gave signs as a witness of His genuine
sending Moses (4:2-9, especially verses 5 and 8).

I can hear you saying, "Yeah, if God would speak di-
rectly to me and assure me with miraculous signs, I
would probably agree to be His tool, too." Signs were
used to authenticate God's messengers when new reve-
lation was to be transmitted through those messengers.
There were three periods when miraculous signs were in
effect: the period of Moses and Joshua, the period of the
prophets (especially Elijah and Elisha), and the period of
Jesus, the apostles, and the New Testament prophets.

Once the people believed Moses, they no longer asked
for signs from him to validate his message. Instead his
message was put into written form, and the people of
God read and quoted from the writing. The same is true
of the prophets. The messages of Elijah and Elisha were
recorded, and the Jews used those written messages as
God's Word to them. The same is true of the founders of
Christianity (Ephesians 2:20). The message of Jesus and
of the New Testament apostles and prophets was authen-
ticated by signs while they were alive, and it was both
passed on orally and put in writing. The question might
come, "What signs were these?" We need only to read
the Gospels and Acts to determine the answer. The
miraculous activities of the apostles and Jesus included
raising the dead, healing the sick, speaking in different
languages, and discerning spirits. We do not have to
guess about the signs of the apostles or the miracles and
wonders which God performed to validate Jesus. Once
we realize what these miracles were and what their use
was, it is not difficult to understand that some of the gifts
listed in 1 Corinthians 12 functioned as foundational gifts
(not continuous) for the church, i.e. confirming Jesus,
apostles, and prophets—the foundation upon which the
church is built (Ephesians 2:20). As the Jews of long ago
passed on the messages of Moses and the prophets that

23

had been confirmed by signs, so we Christians should do that today with the messages of Jesus, the apostles, and the New Testament prophets.

These messages of God have been written down for our use. We are to bring them to bear upon our current situation and to couple them with conduct dedicated to God's ethics and exhortation. (See 1 Peter 1:12-16; 2:12, 24; 3:8-17.) As Moses brought the word of God to both the political and the religious community, so must we.

We must take careful note how Moses approached the political community. He did not do it as a Lone Ranger, nor did he call for a grass roots revolution. He first spoke to the religious leaders as God had instructed (Exodus 3:16; 4:29); the people believed their leaders (4:31). Then the religious leaders aligned with Moses, and together they brought the word of God into the politcal arena (3:18).

There are many implications for us today. No one should bypass the leaders of the Christian community to begin any kind of reformation movement. There is much oppression still around us to which the Christian community needs to speak. However, unless the leaders are convinced that God hates all kinds of oppression, the word of God will have little effect.

Another lesson we can learn is that the Christian community must take a great deal of care in electing her leaders. Leaders who are not spiritually mature will not have the courage to allow God's word to be spoken to the situations of our day. Congregations who do not take seriously the qualifications of leaders in 1 Timothy and Titus are setting themselves against the wisdom of Heaven and are aiming at overruling the dominion of God's government.

Our Task

Indeed the job is difficult, and God is calling all of us to be involved. No Christian is to be exempt. God has shared His blessings with us all, so we can become partners in fulfilling His purposes in the world. We are His ambassadors (2 Corinthians 5:20) and therefore to be active in ending hostilities caused by oppression and replacing them with peace and reconciliation. We are to be God's peacemakers (Matthew 5:9; James 3:18) by bringing the good news of what God has done in Christ to the minds of people so their lives will be transformed and oppression will be stopped.

We must couple our preaching with practice. We must cross the barriers of oppression and associate with and love the oppressed. It will be costly to do it. Neither Moses, Jesus, or Paul was liked by the establishment, and we won't be liked either if we do our job.

There are many corrupt influences in our world today that are enslaving people to the evils around us: violence in movies and television, indecent movies, massage parlors, rampant divorce and remarriage, exploitation by big business, drug traffic, political deceit and bribery, waste of resources, etc. I am convinced that these types of slavery are much worse than the slavery of the Hebrews who had to build cities for the Pharaoh under tough taskmasters. These evils will hurt our children much more than the hard work of the Hebrews hurt their children. We who are God's children with our citizenship in Heaven must say with charity and clarity that we will have nothing to do with corrupt influences and will stand firmly against them.

It is true that we cannot Christianize our society without bringing it to conversion, but we do not need to stand silently by while the unconverted Pharaohs in high and low places enslave our children to taskmasters that lead to an eternal hell. We must have leaders who are committed to God above everything else. Then we must have people who will follow those leaders through the "Red Sea." Let us never forget that God stands on the side of the right.

God needs human tools who will see needs. Do you see needs around you? He needs people who know that He cares. Do you know that Jesus cares about those needs? He needs those who recognize their inadequacies. What are yours? He needs persons who believe that He will help and are committed to allowing God to help through them. That is why Moses was a great leader. Why not be one, too?

3

Let My People Go

Exodus 5-13

Liberators We Must Be

Once Dwight L. Moody heard someone say, "The world has yet to see what Jesus can do through one person totally committed to Him." Moody decided he wanted to be that kind of person. He led several small unwanted boys into real freedom when he began a boys' Sunday-school class in the back of a shoe store. He was not discouraged when he was told that if he wanted a class he would have to get his own members and provide the place for them to meet. Why was he above discouragement? Because he was committed to showing some people what real freedom is. He was saying, "Let my people go." From that meager beginning were born Moody Bible Institute and *Moody Monthly*.

Earl Hargrove wanted to see people released from

shackles in 1944 when nearly a thousand churches in Illinois had locked their doors due to a famine of preachers. Amid much opposition and skepticism, he began Lincoln Bible Institute in Lincoln, Illinois. Even though the people did not believe it, he led the way, saying, "The preachers are coming!" And come they did. Church doors reopened, and Illinois became a leading state in the restoration movement. Earl Hargrove was saying, "Let my people go."

In the 1800's Thomas and Alexander Campbell longed to see the fetters of denominationalism broken. They wanted people to be free from the chains of human opinions and the theological inventions of men. They began a religious movement comprised of people from many different denominational backgrounds who dared to say, "Where the Bible speaks, we speak, and where the Bible is silent, we are silent. In essentials unity, in nonessentials liberty, and in all things love. We have no creed but Christ." The Campbells were saying, "Let my people go."

All of these men were in the likeness of Moses—liberators. Each of them was a leader before he was recognized as one. It is easy for some of us to isolate ourselves from current issues and claim, "I'm not a leader." A leader is one who leads; one becomes a leader by leading. Some claim, "Leaders are born that way." Sure, we are all born. You were born and have the potential of becoming a leader—a leader who can say, "Let my people go."

Of course, we cannot all do fantastic feats as these men who were mentioned, but each of us can be a leader to someone. Parents are to be leaders to their children. Many evil influences are trying to enslave our children. We must have the courage to say, "Let my children go." This type of courage is not being demonstrated very well in our country. School boards, administrators, and teachers are enslaving our children to ungodly philosophies and ideals of education, but we seldom hear the cries of parents for their emancipation.

The mass media with their onslaught of pagan ideas and practices are reaching out to capture the minds of our children. Where are our leaders to cry out and demand freedom for our children?

We cannot wait for a powerful Moses. We have to be leaders ourselves in our own homes and in our communities. We must so live and speak that our children will recognize our leadership and be thankful for it.

Courage in Leadership

Where can we show the courage to be such leaders? Moses had such courage. How did he display it?

First, Moses went to the source of the enslavement he wanted to destroy—the Pharaoh (Exodus 5:1). We too must go the sources of the slavery we want to end. If our children are being oppressed by false philosophies in their schools, then we must go to the school boards with our complaints instead of talking behind their backs. If laws in our communities are inadequate or unfair, then let us go to the sources of these laws to seek changes.

Because the source of all oppression is Satan, we must be constant in evangelism. It is true that institutions and organizations will change policies due to the pressure of the people, but such changes will only last until the next pressure group appears. The source of lasting change is in the reorientation of lives under a new Lord—Jesus.

Second, Moses brought the word from God to the issue he was facing (Exodus 6:29). Although not everyone will receive God's salvation, everyone needs to hear what God has to say about situations of the day. He is the Lord of this universe, and we must speak His word to whoever is in this universe. God's word is not to be cooped up in the church building. It must be brought out into the open in committee meetings, planning sessions, business deals, and legislative sessions. It must be heard around the tables of big business, educational curriculum planning, and governmental lawmaking.

As I write this, the Missouri House of Representatives is considering an amendment to remove sanctions against any deviant sexual behavior between consenting adults. Many are particularly hoping for the decriminalization of homosexuality. One sponsor of the amendment said, "In this code we are trying to get at the problems of the community." What a way to get at problems! He continued that they (lawmakers) do not want to sermonize or moralize citizens. O. L. Wallis, a Christian legislator from Poplar Bluff, Missouri, led in an effort to outlaw all deviant sexual behavior and even to make it a crime to have sexual intercourse with anyone other than a person's marital partner. He was quoted in every major Missouri newspaper as saying, "If we accept deviant behavior, we are doing wrong. This is a violation of the morals of the community. The Scriptures will bear this out."

Now why would this legislator bring the Scriptures to the issue? Because the Scriptures speak out loudly and clearly. Why should Christians allow non-Christian ethics to be the only ones that get a hearing? When we view the enslavement that extramarital sex brings to our society in the form of V.D., illegitimate children, broken homes, and all the ramifications, we must allow the Lord of the universe to be heard! I believe every Christian has the obligation to bring the implications of the Word of God into whatever situation he is involved in (Colossians 3:17).

Third, Moses did not allow questions to sidetrack the word of God (Exodus 5:2). We may find ourselves "chasing rabbits" trying to answer all the questions we are asked. We do not need to know all the reasons why God said something or answer all the questions about who God is. In fact, we are warned not to get caught up in the wisdom of the world (1 Corinthians 1:17-31) and to stay out of questionings and arguments that may sidetrack us from our real purpose (2 Timothy 2:23-26).

One reason parents do not lead their children more decisively concerning what the Word of God says about the current issues is that they are afraid the children will ask a question they cannot answer. One thing we are to know—the reason for the hope we have (1 Peter 3:15), which is the resurrection of Jesus, simple and pure—not all the intellectual, philosophical, sociological, psychological, anthropological, and scientific questions (1 Peter 1:3).

Perhaps you don't even know where to look in the Bible for God's word concerning an issue like homosexuality. Then purchase a complete concordance such as *Young's Analytical Concordance of the Bible* or *Strong's Exhaustive Concordance of the Bible,* keep it in your home, and use it.

In the *fourth* place, Moses did not let false charges detour him (Exodus 5:4, 5). How many times are we silenced by, "You just don't want us to enjoy life. You are trying to stifle the creativity and humanity of people."

Neither did Moses let the complaints of the people he was trying to help stop him (Exodus 5:20-23; 6:9). It is tough when the very people you are trying to help see you as a threat to them. I'm sure many people are against the position of Missouri legislator O. L. Wallis; yet his legislation is intended to help the very people who do not want it.

Moses would not give up. He went to the Pharaoh seven times (Exodus 5:1; 7:16; 8:1, 20; 9:1, 13; 10:1), repeating, "Let my people go." He did not allow false promises to steer him off his course. Four times the Pharaoh tried to get Moses off his back by promising that changes would take place (8:8, 25; 9:27, 28; 10:8). Moses was not interested in a verbal promise but in practices that supported it.

Fifth, Moses would not compromise. Three times Pharaoh tried to meet Moses partway, but it was not enough for Moses (Exodus 8:26-29; 10:8-11; 10:24-26).

31

Moses was not playing football where both sides meet on the fifty-yard line. He was sharing the word of the Lord, which is absolute and "not for hire." He did not allow fake confession and counterfeit repentance to fool him (Exodus 9:27; 10:16). Twice the Pharaoh confessed that he had sinned, but Moses would not relent until the Pharaoh's deeds showed repentance.

Moses' persistence with the Pharaoh and patience with the people resulted in liberation for the Hebrews. At times Moses doubted and wondered if it was worth the effort (Exodus 6:12, 30). But he kept before him the goal of freedom for the oppressed. He looked beyond the pressures, opposition, and lack of appreciation. He was determined to accomplish his goal even if it cost him his life. Through it all, he finally emerged as a recognized leader. In Exodus 2 we read that he was not recognized as leader. "Who made you a prince or judge over us?" (2:14). Then we read in 11:3, "Moses himself was greatly esteemed in the land of Egypt, both in the sight of Pharaoh's servants and in the sight of the people."

What made the difference? In chapter 2, he took matters into his own hands and handled them in accordance with his own way, and then ran. In contrast, in chapters 5 through 13 he put matters into God's hands and did things God's way, and emerged as a leader. Deciding to do things God's way will also enable us to say with courage, "Let my people go."

Jesus also exemplified courageous leadership. He came to set people free (Luke 4:18-21), as the word *redemption* implies. He went to the source of oppression—Satan—and declared our freedom. He brought God's word to bear on current situations. He refused to be sidetracked by trying to answer all the questions asked him (Matthew 21:23-27). He never allowed false charges to detour Him. People accused Him of having a demon, of being crazy, and of being a Samaritan (Matthew 12:24; Mark 3:21; John 8:48). The fact that

He was rejected by the very ones He came to help did not stop Him (John 1:11). He did not compromise (Matthew 4:1-11), and He did not allow false confession to fool him (Matthew 7:21; Luke 18:18-23). He was even deserted at one time by His disciples (Matthew 26:56), but even then He did not falter. As Moses, Jesus did things God's way and was a great leader because of it.

Only with this kind of leadership can we be used to free others from the oppression that threatens. Much of our evangelism fails because we lack the leadership qualities that we have just discussed. We must confront Satan and the evil of the oppression; we must apply God's Word to present-day situations. We must have His goal ahead of us and not be sidetracked from it. We must not allow what others say about us to stop us, nor be discouraged by criticism. We must not compromise; we must not be fooled by false confessions and repentance. We must proceed and remain in God's way to free the world eternally.

Some may say we could be more effective and powerful if we could use miraculous signs to convince others of God's way and word as Moses did. Each one of the plagues God directed through Moses challenged one or more of the gods worshiped by the Egyptians. For instance, darkness challenged the effectiveness of their sun god, Re; the Nile turning to blood challenged the effectiveness of the Nile-god, Hapi; the frogs challenged the effectiveness of their goddess, Hequit. God used the plagues to demonstrate to the people that He was indeed God (Exodus 9:16; 8:10, 22).

Christians have been given a sign to point people to the power of God, and we also have the power to demonstrate the reality of God. That sign is the resurrection. Every time people asked Jesus for a sign, He always pointed to the resurrection (Matthew 12:39, 40; Luke 11:29, 30).

The power we have received to demonstrate the reality

of God is the Holy Spirit, who unites us to the likeness of God. We demonstrate God by living lives that show the ineffectiveness of the "gods" other people are following. May our love, joy, peace, patience, kindness, goodness, faithfulness, gentleness, and self-control outdo anything their "gods" of slavery can do. Only then will they be willing to be freed from the bonds of their slavery to become free men in Christ. Our demand, "Let my people go," must be backed by our remaining in God's way with His Word.

As the liberation of the Hebrews was to be remembered by a Passover feast, so is ours. Our "Passover feast" is the Lord's Supper, our regular reminder that Jesus is our Passover lamb. His death has made our freedom possible. To know Jesus is to acknowledge that whenever the cry, "Let my people go," is followed by an exodus from any form of slavery, then God was active through the lives of certain leaders. Let us be those leaders!

4

Celebration of Freedom

Exodus 14, 15

The Exodus

Freedom is tough. It is tough to become freed, and it is tough to live in freedom. The oppressor is reluctant to release the captives, and the enslaved are reluctant to be freed. The hesitancy for both comes from the same reason—dependency on security. The oppressor has depended on the slaves to provide his security, and the slaves have learned to depend upon their masters for their necessities.

Moses encountered this reluctance for freedom. Both Pharaoh and the enslaved people complained and wanted to reverse the process that would lead to emancipation (Exodus 14:5, 11). The same reluctance is apparent in our enslaved relationships. Even in our own country when the slaves were to be freed, some masters did not want to free the slaves, and some slaves did not want to leave the security their masters had provided.

A religion that enslaves people does not wish to release them. At the same time, people who fight for religious freedom often return to the kind of oppression they left. They feel more secure in the "old ways."

In the first century many Jews who had converted to Christianity had a difficult time becoming liberated from Judaism. The new converts felt more secure keeping the laws of Judaism.

This same reluctance is seen when people seek to be free of sin. Satan does not give up easily. Not only will he put up a struggle to block the release of the sinner, but he will use his "captains" as did the Pharaoh of Egypt. Those who help Satan enslave people to sin—the drug pushers, the Mafia, the distilleries, the cigaret manufacturers, the pornography pushers, the tavern owners, the madams and pimps, etc.—will use any kind of strategy to keep customers. Satan will even use our friends and companions to lure us to stay in sin.

No, it is not easy to make an exodus from the slavery of sin. Recognizing the slavery is a positive step. Then turning from sin and beginning to walk another way is essential—this is called repentance. As soon as a person takes a step toward freedom, he may begin to have second thoughts. The Hebrew people did (Exodus 14:12), and so will you. Some kind of "Red Sea" will be facing you, causing you to wonder why you wanted to leave the security of your dependency. New responsibilities will face you, and it may look as if the barrier is uncrossable.

As you stand there seeking to face up to the new life that is ahead of you, your former life will torment you. It may get very tough. For the Hebrews, the Red Sea was ahead of them with no bridges or boats in sight, while the Pharaoh was out to get them from behind. They were thinking they should surrender to Pharaoh and forget all about freedom (Exodus 14:12). You may be thinking you should surrender to your old life of sin and forget about trying a new and different way of life.

Sometimes the persecution of your past life is a blessing to you. Sometimes that is just what you need to push onward. You may soon see that your former companions never really cared for you, but only for themselves. Problems can help you decide to trust in the faithfulness of God (1 Peter 1:3-9).

In such a situation, it is imperative that you listen to Christian leaders (Exodus 14:13). The advice they give may not sound logical, but they have been through life with God. They see things from the viewpoint of Christian maturity. Enslavement to sin probably has put certain blinders on your eyes.

If you are truly determined to turn from the oppression of sin and live a new life of freedom; then confess your faith in God and cross the "Red Sea"—which is baptism by immersion. Paul referred to the Hebrews' crossing of the sea as their baptism, recorded for our example (1 Corinthians 10:1, 2). In this act freedom is secured, and the exodus is finally accomplished.

Freedom Is Secured

Now that freedom is secured, the new life begins, accompanied by some real dangers. One danger is attempting to tackle too much. I have known immature Christians who have decided to fight battles they were not ready for—street evangelism, prison evangelism, foreign mission work, etc. God recognized that this would be dangerous for the Hebrews and did not allow them to travel where they would be in battle soon (Exodus 13:17). Battles would have to come, but God knew they needed both verbal guidelines and some time spent maturing under their leaders. New Christians must recognize their infant status and humbly grow with other Christians while feeding upon God's written Word.

Another danger that faced the Hebrews in their new life

was the possibility of their wandering aimlessly through the wilderness (Exodus 14:3). The same danger faces a new Christian. With no goals, aims, or attachments, he may just wander around. But God has provided a way to combat this danger. When you are freed from sin, you are to become attached to the church—God's community. Without the stability, growth, goals, and activities provided by the church, you will not make it to the "promised land." There is no place for individual independence and arrogance in freedom; we need each other as we all travel in our new life.

These dangers are not to be dwelled upon. Instead the newly freed person must immediately celebrate his freedom by worshiping positively with thanksgiving and joy, for his freedom is a gift from God. The Hebrews celebrated their freedom by praising God, promising God, hoping for the future, and merrymaking. Who said merrymaking is not to be part of the Christian life? (Exodus 15:20).

Worship is a celebration. Baptism and the Lord's Supper especially ought to be surrounded with the air of celebration. We often look so sad during communion that visitors are sure to think Jesus is still dead. What would be wrong with singing "Joy to the World" during the Lord's Supper? We must be more positive when participating in these ordinances. For instance, why is the baptismal dressing room the most depressing room in the church building? Why not decorate it to communicate the joy involved in baptism?

Notice the three elements of the Hebrew's song of celebration (Exodus 15:1-18): (1) Praise to God—"He is highly exalted . . . the Lord is my strength and song, and He has become my salvation; this is . . . my Father's God . . . Thy right hand, O Lord, is majestic in power." Then come many verses telling what He has done. Their words were similar to our songs of praise—"How Great Thou Art," "A Mighty Fortress Is Our God." (2) Promises to

God—"I will praise Him . . . I will extol Him." These are like our song, "I Love to Tell the Story." (3) Hoping for the future—"Thou wilt bring them and plant them in the mountain of Thine inheritance, the place, O Lord, which Thou hast made for thy dwelling." That is like our song, "When We All Get to Heaven."

But positive words are not enough. Positive works must accompany them. Celebration for what God has done must be coupled with a commitment to what we will do. Sunday singing must be followed by Monday serving.

Three days after the celebration of the greatness of God, the Hebrews grumbled (Exodus 15:24)—a common human characteristic. How can we insure that our celebration does not end at the close of the worship service? Moses' advice to the Hebrews is helpful to us also: "Give earnest heed to the voice of the Lord your God, and do what is right in His sight, and give ear to His commandments, and keep all His statutes" (Exodus 15:26).

5

Commitment to a Covenant

Exodus 19, 20; Deuteronomy 10—12

God's purpose for granting a people freedom has never changed—"For you were called to freedom, brethren; only do not turn your freedom into an opportunity for the flesh, but through love serve one another" (Galatians 5:13). God frees us to be a blessing to others.

But how could a people who for generations had been dependent upon others for the care of their needs take on the responsibility themselves? They had been accustomed to being dependent; now they were to become interdependent—needing each other. That's the rub. How does a group turn into a community (common oneness)? When Moses inherited the Hebrew people, he had a potential time bomb on his hands. Here were millions of people who had not been used to caring for one another. How would they get along?

Just three days after they were freed, the security of their slavery gone, the Hebrews began to grumble at Moses (Exodus 15:24). Grumbling at leaders is the first step toward grumbling at and distrusting one another. Paul said it well: "If you bite and devour one another, take care lest you be consumed by one another" (Galatians 5:15). How can we make sure this does not happen? Paul also said, "For the whole Law is fulfilled in one word, in the statement, 'You shall love your neighbor as yourself' " (Galatians 5:14).

That word is so familiar to us that we sometimes quote it glibly without realizing what it is to love a neighbor. The law is not fulfilled by merely saying we love; we must love "in deed and truth" (1 John 3:18). Love is seen in deeds when we help the weak (1 Thessalonians 5:14), when we regard others as better than ourselves and look out for their interests as well as our own (Philippians 2:3, 4), when we do good to all people, especially to our fellow Christians (Galatians 6:10). Christian love is not a warm personal feeling reserved for those who love us in return. It is a cordial and active goodwill extended even to those who hate us. "Love your enemies," said Jesus, "do good to those who hate you" (Luke 6:27). Jesus himself set the example: "Greater love has no one than this, that one lay down his life for his friends" (John 15:13). And He did that for us while we were yet sinners (Romans 5:8).

Paul's teachings give us a clue as to why it was important that the Hebrews receive the law. God's law was given partly to communicate the content of love—practical ways to care for one another. It was needed to protect the people from their own self-destruction. The law was given to function as guardrails along their highway of life. The law could keep them on the right road until they would reach the position that God intended them to reach. That position of maturity would be shown by their caring for one another, not because of the outside pressure of the law but because of their inside de-

41

sire. That time would come with Jesus who would share His life with them (Galatians 3:21-25).

God spoke about that new position through Jeremiah:

> I will make a new covenant with the house of Israel and with the house of Judah, not like the covenant which I made with their fathers in the day I took them by the hand to bring them out of the land of Egypt. . . . But this is the covenant which I will make with the house of Israel after those days . . . I will put My law within them, and on their heart I will write it   —Jeremiah 31:31-33.

The law was the guardian and manager to protect and guide the Hebrews who were in a state of childhood until they could reach "adulthood" in Jesus (Galatians 4:1-5).

We parents use this same principle with our children today. We do not allow little children who have been freed from the dependency of the mother's womb to treat their brothers and sisters the way they want to. Instead we make rules to guide them. If we did not, they would become savages. Our rules demonstrate to them the content of love before they even know what the word "love" means.

In the covenant relationship between God and the Hebrews established on Mount Sinai, the people could become savages or saints (holy) in the wilderness. God's love directed them toward the latter choice. God wanted them to advance from freedom (Exodus 19:4) to becoming a kingdom of priests and a holy nation (19:6). The route was for them to live within the guardrails that God had erected for their good (19:5).

This is the content that God spoke to Moses, that Moses spoke to the elders, and that the elders spoke to the people. The people committed themselves to this covenant (19:7, 8). They agreed to be identified both with the privileges of God, "you shall be My own possession" (19:5), and with the purposes of God, "a kingdom of priests" (19:6). And those of us who have been freed from sin, as we enter God's family, agree to receive the gift of salvation and the responsibilities of service.

The covenant-agreement between God and the Hebrews was not an agreement between equals, as are many secular agreements (seller and buyer). God did not consult with the people before He outlined the covenant. He is God and He knows what is best for His people; His covenant was for their good. It was not for the people to argue about or alter. It was for either their acceptance or their rejection.

It is the same with God's new covenant in Jesus. It is not a covenant between equals. We have no right to argue about it or ignore portions of it that we do not like. We must accept all of it or none of it. We are not to alter any terms of salvation or to make them more "relevant" for our changing times. Yes, times do change; but God's new covenant does not.

What if we don't like the necessity of repentance or of immersion for salvation? Tough. We are to obey. God did not lay before us a smorgasbord for us to pick and choose what we like; His covenant comes in one package. To disobey one part of it is to disobey the whole. Paul quoted, "Cursed is everyone who does not abide by all the things written in the book of the Law, to perform them" (Galatians 3:10). James said, "For whoever keeps the whole law and yet stumbles in one point, he has become guilty of all" (James 2:10).

Jesus came to give us a new covenant because the old could not save but only guide (Galatians 2:16). When we are immersed, we put on Christ; putting on Christ is putting on His Spirit. That Spirit produces in our lives the kind of life against which there is no law (Galatians 5:22, 23). Through the activity of the Spirit we receive the character to live out the intentions of the law—to love God and our fellowmen.

Even when we receive the character to live out God's

kind of love, we need to know the content of that love. The Christian *wants* to love, but how is he to know what actions are not love? That is why we have the teachings of the New Testament. While the law given to the Hebrews at Sinai looked forward to Christ, the teachings given to Christians in the writings of the New Testament apostles and prophets look back to Christ. The Hebrews could only proceed toward Christ; we are growing *in* Him.

The old and new covenants have two things in common: both demand that the holiness and absolute authority of God be recognized and honored (Exodus 20:1-7; Matthew 22:37, 38) and both demand the dignity of fellowmen be recognized and honored (Exodus 20:12-17; Matthew 22:39). The law at Mount Sinai is fulfilled by the new covenant when we are in Christ, love God as He loved Him, and love our fellowmen as God does.

True freedom is found when we become functioning members of God's covenant—the covenant of caring out of faith, love, and hope, all of which are possible because of God's grace.

6

The Necessity of Worship

Exodus 33:1—36:1

Togetherness

Just agreeing to a covenant will not insure our faithfulness to that covenant. Many influences seek to pull us back to the old form of slavery. It is one thing to hear our children agree to the principles we know are good for them. It is quite another thing to watch them leave for school, social events, or work where they will spend time under the influence of others who may not share our principles. A daily family reunion of the scattered members is a must. Not only should a family pray together to stay together, but they should also meet together, eat together, and play together. The gathering of the family unit better insures faithfulness to the past heritage and to the present members of that family. Such get-togethers also insure the continuation of the values of that family.

When these "meetings" of the family are dropped, lack of commitment, discontinuity, and lack of communication come on the scene. One of the disadvantages of our mobile society is this fragmentation of the family unity which results in the vagueness of the family ideals. I have not been to one family reunion. I do not know my cousins by name, nor have I seen my aunts or uncles in twenty years. It has been that long since I have seen my aunt who lives in my home town, population six thousand. It has been a long time since my three sisters and myself have been together at the same time. What a tragedy! Consequently, no one could recognize among my aunts, uncles, cousins, sisters, and myself a similarity of heritage and values. When there is no getting together, a family is a family in name only.

It works the same way within God's family. We must not only be ready to agree to the covenant with the right words; we must also be prepared to meet with others who agree with the covenant. A covenant with words must be accompanied by a community with worship. Because of the many influences that can pull us apart from one another and from a commitment to our common heritage and values, we need to meet together. These meetings are not optional; they are essential.

The distance that exists between family members who live in the same town can also exist between the members of God's family, no matter what the size. Television is not a helpful influence; it tends to keep us away from the gathering of God's people. The Sunday morning religious programs may prove to be bad influences upon Christianity, for some people have substituted them for meeting with others in worship. There is no legitimate substitute for the gathering of God's people.

God knew that the Hebrews who had committed themselves to His covenant would always need to meet with one another. If they did not, they would become remote from one another and submit to the influences of others around them (Exodus 34:12-17). Every week there was to be "a holy convocation" (Leviticus 23:3). The men of the whole nation were to meet together three times a year (Exodus 34:23). Can you imagine what the North American Christian Convention would be like if it were a worldwide convention that met three times a year, and every Christian male were expected to attend? The Hebrews learned the value of that kind of corporate togetherness. We Christians have not even begun to understand the value of it. We often hear the complaint, "The convention is getting too big." When will it dawn upon us why the Hebrew nation did not lose its identity or distinctiveness in those threatening days?

The Hebrews did not argue about whether or not they should build a meeting place, as some Christians do today. God commanded that a meeting place be provided (Exodus 35:4-19). There was no disputing about the design of the building or about the material. God supplied the plan, and the people followed it. Everything was made according to the pattern (Exodus 25:40).

Everyone helped and shared. Some brought raw materials; some brought their possessions that could be melted into the metals that were needed. Women spun material and brought finished products. Some brought spice and oil for lighting and incense (Exodus 35:20-29). They also provided the skilled labor to fashion the materials into a meeting place. Designers, cutters of stone, carvers of wood, engravers, weavers, and seamstresses joined together in the construction of the sanctuary (35:30—36:1).

The Hebrews were committed to meet together, and they supported that commitment with their giving. From the beginning of their covenant relationship with God, they took seriously their responsibility to assemble together. But their meetings were not just people-oriented; they were also God-oriented. They met to worship the God who had freed them from slavery. It was because of what God had done that they were a distinctive people. They knew that the continuation of their distinctiveness depended partly upon their rehearsing for themselves and their children the wonderful deeds of God (Deuteronomy 6:6-9). They passed on from generation to generation the family's relationship to God.

It must also be this way with us in both our genetic families and our spiritual family. God's family is just one generation away from becoming extinct due to lack of evangelism or lack of corporate worship to remember and celebrate His mighty acts.

God's program for keeping His family distinct has never changed. His strategy is for those equipped with God's Word to equip others to become leaders with His Word. Those leaders equip the parents, and the parents equip their children. Whenever that chain is broken in any link, there will arise a generation of children not equipped with God's Word. Those children will grow up to be leaders, but they will be the wrong kind. Are we experiencing a breakdown in that chain today? Which link is weak? The breakdown is obvious when the number of members of our churches is compared with the number of worshipers. The picture even looks bleaker when we consider that the number of members is mainly adults, while a large percentage of the worshipers are children and non-member adults.

We must convince one another of the imperative of worship, not that it is just for our individual salvation (selfish level), but that it is the corporate responsibility of being a covenant people who belong to the family of God. What we do or do not do affects all the generations of Christians after us and the whole of Christianity with us.

The practical reasons for regular worship are many. In worship God's Word is rehearsed. We are brought face to face again with His holiness. Our selfhood is exposed as we see ourselves for what we are and what we can be-

48

come. We see our world for what it is and for what it can become. We are challenged to confront the world with God. The gathering of the Christian community strengthens us to stay out of sin. How many times have you detoured from sin because of the hurt it would bring to your Christian brothers and sisters? Or because of the possibility of having to leave the Christian community if you remain in sin?

A close-knit family that spends time together has a definite disciplinary value. We can correct one another and admonish one another. The togetherness of moral people deters moral delinquency.

The day I began writing this chapter, our local newspaper released an article about the instructor at the county jail. Of the 103 persons she had taught there, 101 of them were from broken homes. I talked to a friend, Judge Herbert Casteel of Carthage, Missouri, who said two-thirds of the people on probation or parole he works with are from broken homes. This does not just apply to youth. One study reveals that unmarried men are many times more likely to be in jail or prison than married men. Attachments do help prevent delinquency.

The closer the members of a group are to one another, the more they realize how much they need each other and the more they understand that they cannot make it on the weekly battlefield alone. We need the support of all of the other Christian "soldiers." Separation from the family due to continued sin is spiritual suicide.

Another value in fellowshiping together in worship is the stimulation and encouragement we receive from one another (Hebrews 10:24, 25). Our freedom brings new attachments—to God and to others who belong to God. The closer we draw to God in worship, the closer we draw to others who worship Him. But to participate in this closeness, we must meet together. That is why it is important that congregations meet with other congregations from time to time.

The Worship Service

I am afraid, however, that many of our worship services separate and alienate us. It is not the "worship" that does it, but our attitudes toward certain parts of the service. We often spend more time evaluating and criticizing the forms of the service than actually worshiping. We spend a lot of time reading the order of worship in the bulletin to find out what comes next. Sometimes we may be looking to see how long it will be till it is over.

The Word of God does not dictate what the order of the worship service should be, nor where we should worship, nor the hour, nor the length of the service, nor how many songs we should sing, nor whether we should have the Lord's Supper before or after the sermon, nor who should serve it. The Bible does not even say we have to sing an invitation hymn each time; I rather doubt that one was sung at all during the first century. Isn't it ironic (and sad) that a freed people have fettered worship to their own ways?

It would not be heresy for a worship service to begin with the congregation on their knees, or a Scripture reading, or special music, or even a baptism. It would not be wrong to have a responsive reading out of the Bible instead of using the back of the hymnal. Many have discovered that people worship with more openness and expectancy if the "order of worship" is not printed in the bulletin.

Preachers have been fired for changing the order of worship. That fact alone convinces me that we ought to have enough change from time to time to prevent us from becoming slaves to an order of worship. What a farce worship becomes when it is bound and fettered to our ways of doing things instead of dedicated to remembering God's ways and His Word.

May our worship services never alienate, but mold us into the kinds of people God knows we can become. May we worship God—together.

7

Living It Out

Numbers 13, 14

Day by Day Walk

Becoming a people of God is a result of the freedom God gives, but *being* a people of God is not fulfilled merely by accepting that freedom, agreeing to His covenant, or calling Him "Lord" in corporate worship. "Not everyone who says to me, 'Lord, Lord' will enter the kingdom of heaven, but he who does the will of my Father who is in heaven," stated Jesus (Matthew 7:21). God said the same thing to the Hebrews: "If you will indeed obey My voice . . ." (Exodus 19:5). Being a people of God calls for a day-by-day walk with God; it is the keeping of His covenant, which calls for continual commitment.

When the covenant is broken, it is easy to cover up the break with an external show of faithfulness, as is done in many interpersonal covenants. A man and woman pledge to one another before witnesses that they will love, honor, and respect one another "in joy and in sorrow, in prosperity and in adversity, for better or worse." Such a promise calls for day-by-day devotion and mutual care; but that devotion can wane without many knowing it. It is not too difficult to keep up the externals. He comes home every night and pays the bills. She keeps the house and prepares the meals. They both attend church; the children are active in Little League and school activities. A couple can work harder at keeping up the externals than at seeking to eradicate the decay that exists on the inside. They begin to think that keeping up the externals is all that is needed to keep their promise to one another. It then becomes difficult to love and care for each other day by day.

This can happen in God's family also. Our day-by-day walk may become halting, but we can cover it up by keeping up the externals—going to church, giving our offering, doing committee work. We can easily expend more energy maintaining the externals than cleaning up the decay that lies on the inside. It will not be long before we begin thinking that we are acceptable to God as long as we carry out our institutional responsibilities.

Professional Christian workers are not immune to this malady. It is easy to feel that all is O.K. as long as we meet our preaching, teaching, and calling assignments, as long as we show up at the meetings on time, as long as we turn out a Christian product at the end of a day of full-time Christian involvement. There is a book entitled *How to Be a Christian Without Being Religious.* Someone could easily write a book entitled *How to Be Religious Without Being a Christian.*

Let's face reality. There are many situations in which it is harder to fulfill our commitment to God than it is to keep up the external show. It is hard to apply the principle of forgiveness when one's husband or wife has been caught in adultery or when someone raises an erroneous complaint against you. How can we be long-suffering when the light has barely turned green and the fellow behind us is lying on the horn? How can we not gossip with our closest friend when we have just heard the juiciest story? How gentle can we be when the umpire in the Little League game makes a wrong call against our boy? How successful are we men in "tearing out the eye" (Matthew 5:29) when a beauty bends over and exposes herself? Or how hospitable are we when a college choir comes to stay the night? Do we seek our own way at the board meetings? Can we be content with what we have? Can we stay away from arguments and quarrels about God's law? How do we feel when a barefoot child walks into the worship service? Do we get upset when foreigners or blacks move in next door?

Are we obeying our leaders and submitting to them? Husbands, are you loving your wives the way Christ loves the church, or are you trying to be a dictator? Wives, are you submitting to your husbands, or are you heeding the tenets of the women's liberationists and seeking to think and act independently of him? Children, are you honoring and obeying your moms and dads, or are you complaining and living the way you want to?

How are we doing at work? Are we doing our very best as if we were working for the Creator, or are we just barely meeting the assembly quota, taking long coffee breaks, and calling in sick when we are not? Do we write personal letters on company time or use the Wats line to make personal calls?

Yes, the day-by-day walk with God is a walk in His ways through sickness and health, joy and sorrow, prosperity and adversity; and forsaking all other ways until we die or He comes again. This is what it means to live out the covenant, and this kind of living cannot be simulated by keeping up the externals. It's a walk of faith and love and hope.

Committees of Rebellion

God promised the Hebrews that He would bring them to the promised land (Exodus 3:17); they had the covenant to help them become a community and the worship to keep them faithful and distinct. The externals were there, but something happened that greatly impeded their progress.

The old adage, "a people cannot rise above their leaders" rang true. Many of the leaders were not good examples in their trust, courage, and commitment to God. When God told them to enter the new land (Deuteronomy 1:21), the people decided to form a committee (Deuteronomy 1:22) and God permitted it (Numbers 13:2). But the fact that God permitted it does not mean He sanctioned it. When God says something should be done, we have no right to form a committee to investigate and vote on whether or not to do it. That process often leads to rebellion against the command of the Lord.

It is not right to have an elected committee of the church or a selected committee of our friends to decide about moral issues. The committee may say, "It won't hurt"; "Everybody's doing it"; "Be courageous, don't be a party-pooper"; "That is old-fashioned, keep up with the times"; "God did not mean it that way"; "You should get a divorce"; "Social drinking does no harm"; "That's one part of big business."

When will we learn that we cannot permit a majority vote to decide on issues when we have a "thus saith the Lord" in the Bible?

No group of leaders has a right to vote "yes" or "no" on a direct command of God. They are only to lead the people to follow that command. Leaders ought to be committed to God's way and trust Him more than human logic or earthly evidence. The majority of the leaders on the Hebrew committee were not so committed to God's way (Deuteronomy 1:23-33). They came back from their survey with a pessimistic view that scared the people

(Numbers 13:23-29). Only two on the committee said they should go and take possession of the land. What would you do if the vote was ten against two, especially when you have decided on a democracy (rule by the people) instead of a theocracy (rule by God)? You would decide the majority was right.

What was wrong with such a committee? They simply did not trust God (Deuteronomy 1:32, Numbers 14:11). They looked out for themselves and decided on their own. How could such men become the leaders? There were no criteria for their selection; they were probably chosen by their popularity.

God does not want us to use that approach, so He gave us guidelines to use in the selection of our leaders (1 Timothy 3:1-13; Titus 1:5-11). The nominating committee in a church dare not say, "God's qualifications are too tough for this day and age," and then nominate someone who simply attends all the services. Often we do not even think of whom we will nominate until just a few weeks before election; then we hurry to prepare a slate of candidates and do not spend the time necessary to evaluate men by God's criteria.

Is it possible that we spend less time considering the background of a prospective preacher than we would the background of a janitor of a bank? Do we spend more time discussing salary and parsonage considerations than talking about doctrinal beliefs? Have we ever drafted people to become teachers just because "someone has to do it?" Is just anyone suitable to fulfill responsibilities in the church simply because he is available? I personally knew of one congregation whose chairman of the evangelism committee was a non-Christian!

It may be that the Hebrews themselves did not want to enter the land at this time and chose leaders who would cater to their wishes (Deuteronomy 1:22). It is an overthrow of God's government to select leaders who will cater to our wishes. How many times has pressure by the people of God changed the right decisions leaders would have made? Leaders who cater to the people start a cycle of immature actions. The Hebrews selected "their own kind" as leaders; the leaders brought back the report the people wanted to hear, and God's word was not heeded.

God hated what had happened to the Hebrews in this instance and declared that none of them, except the two faithful leaders, would enter into the promised land (Deuteronomy 1:35-39). If they would not follow God's way, then they would suffer the aimless wandering in the wilderness (Deuteronomy 1:40).

But again the people took matters into their own hands. They decided to storm the promised land. They were out to prove God wrong. At first they did not have the simple and humble trust to act with no more evidence than the word of God; then they had the arrogance to think they could do it without Him. No wonder God said, "How long will this people spurn Me? And how long will they not believe in Me, despite all the sign which I have performed in their midst?" (Numbers 14:11).

This portion of Hebrew history is usually taught as a nice factual Sunday-school lesson—boring. But it is quite a challenging lesson. It challenges us to take care whom we choose as leaders. It challenges us to beware of simple majority votes, for the majority is not always correct. It challenges us to evaluate why we may be wandering aimlessly without progress.

It challenges us to take a careful look at what it means to have a day-by-day walk with God and to do it regardless of the opposition. We must not be misled by those who say, "It is not the practical way to live." If God says it will work, it will. It teaches us anew that freedom is not the right to do as we please, but to please to do what is right. When that freedom is abused, it may be withdrawn.

The Hebrew people who had little faith in God, but much faith in themselves, failed to inherit the promises of God's covenant. They worked more on the external trappings than on their internal decline and decay. Certainly, *being* a people of God means to live out in faith and practice God's covenant. May we be His children walking in His ways.

8

Light in the Darkness

Joshua 3—6; 14:1-5

A Revival

Will Rogers once said, "Cattle are so cheap that cowboys are eating beef for the first time." God's people have often rallied after rebellion against God to declare, "God's ways are so good that we have decided to walk in them."

Setbacks in progressing with God do not need to destroy us. In fact, they can help us see and correct our mistakes. We do not need setbacks for that purpose, but we can use them to that end.

The Hebrews voted against doing things God's way, and they spent forty years in aimless wandering because of it. But that did not annihilate them. The children grew up to make better decisions than the parents had made. While the committee of the parents had a negative outlook, the committee sent by their children years later had a positive outlook (Joshua 2:1, 24). While the parents would not listen to their leader Moses (Numbers 14:2), the children listened to their leader, Joshua (Joshua 3:1-5). While the parents accepted God's covenant but not His promises (Exodus 19:8), the children accepted both (Joshua 1:16). While the parents chose twelve men to testify against the power of God, the children chose twelve to testify for God's might (Deuteronomy 1:22-26; Joshua 4:20-24).

How could rebellion turn into a revival in one generation? It was not just that the older generation had died, but that they had planted the right positive seeds in the minds of their children. Those years of wandering were not totally wasted. Even though the people were being disciplined, they did not wholly and without interruption turn their backs on God. Although they strayed often, they learned from their mistakes and taught their children not to repeat them. The parents had grumbled time and time again, but they realized their mistakes enough of the time so that not all of their attitudes were transferred to their children.

However, we need to give most of the credit for the revival to Moses and Aaron. They were leaders who would not allow the complaining people to pull them down. The children saw a steady ray of light among these leaders, while the parents only gave off flashes of light now and then.

Moses must be commended for what He did as recorded in the book of Deuteronomy. He rehearsed the history of God with the Hebrews, with a heavy stress on the legislation God had given to Israel nearly forty years before. It was not just boring repetition; Moses adapted the law to the new settled life in the promised land.

He made it clear that the past mistakes were behind them, their inheritance was before them, and God was with them. He stressed the lordship of God who brought them into freedom and who demanded exclusive devotion and worship. Moses brought the realization to them that faith must be married to obedience for the birth and growth of blessings.

But we must not forget that Moses could not have gotten a hearing if the parents had turned their children against him. Somehow, even amid the parents' many times of disobedience, they taught their children to listen to and obey Moses (Joshua 1:17)—an amazing result of the wilderness wanderings.

Our Wilderness

We can learn from this example that life does not have to get worse because we are going through "wilderness wanderings." Today we are wandering in the wilderness of what to do with unwanted babies—kill them or let them live? What are we to do with criminals—execute them or rehabilitate them? What are we to do with Christianity—isolate it from all secularity or let people express their faith in Christ? What are we to do with a marriage that has cooled—shut it off or heat it up? What are we to do with violence in the schools—allow it to continue or stop it? What are we to do with discipline—lighten it or tighten it? What are we to do with deviant sexual activities—legalize them or condemn them? What are we to do with immoral textbooks—burn them or use them? What are we to do with X-rated entertainment—close it down or allow it on prime time on television? What are we to do with sex differences—accept them or strive for uni-sexuality? The wilderness is gigantic, and the wanderings are aimless.

What kind of children can result from such wanderings? That depends largely upon the steady rays of light they can see emanating from Christian leaders who will not be silenced, and the flashes of light from the populace that communicates, "We have not given up and we won't; there is a better way, and we intend to share it." A little light can be seen a long way in the middle of a darkened wilderness.

In the dark wilderness of deteriorating public-school conditions in this country, some lights are being lit. The darkness is seen in vandalism on a massive scale, open drug use, violence between students and teachers, and a deterioration in reading and writing skills. Birch Bayh's Senate subcommittee investigation into this wilderness has had shocking results. It found that there were ten student deaths by drug overdose in one year in the small community of High Ridge, Missouri. Two hundred fifty-one teachers and administrators in the Los Angeles area received serious physical assaults in one year from students. In Philadelphia, 278 students were assaulted by other students in one year.

But some rays of light are beginning to appear, as in Cabool, Missouri, where the school has discontinued the use of *Time* and *Newsweek* because they contained harmful articles. Who complained? The parents! Cabool citizens are not impressed with moral liberalism, regardless of its "respectable" source. Their light is getting attention, too.

Our Revival

We must continually remind our children where we have been with God (history) and where we can go with Him (future). We must never allow the present to so dominate us that the activities of God in the past fade away. In Joshua's day the monument that reminded the people of God's actions was twelve stones (Joshua 4:20-24). In our day, the monuments are God's ordinances and God's church. God has helped us and will continue to do so—and our children need to know it.

Our children also need to see us being used by God to bring some of the wilderness wandering to an end. No, life does not have to get worse because we have made some mistakes and are wandering around trying to find a way out. We can follow God's leading from now on, and if we do it faithfully we can take our children with us. We can influence friends and neighbors, and have an impact on the life of the community. When we follow God we are on the direct route to the promised land.

If we do not break through the walls that keep the evil "Jerichos" standing, perhaps our children will. But if they do, they must do it with faith and obedience in the Word of God. They cannot think it will be done by the modern techniques of psychology, sociology, or philosophy. It may sound illogical to most that God's Word and His way are the answer and the passports through the walls to the "promised land." But it is true. Shortcuts must give way to service, cowardice to courage, and laziness to loyalty. May it be that "God's ways are so good that His people have decided to walk in them."

9

Empty Revival

Judges 1—3

Necessity of Teaching

We can't keep talking about a revival of the good old days. A revival does not automatically keep up its momentum; it requires continuous follow-up. The Hebrew children reversed many of their parents' practices in the wilderness, but time marches on. History is linear. If that reversal was to have any ongoing effect, it had to be continued in the lives of their children, the grandchildren of those who first wandered in the wilderness.

A generation must not only consider what it has improved from the past, but also what it is pouring into the next generation. This is true even in our genetic families. It is possible for all the children of a particular family to get more involved in Christian activities than their parents did. But it is also possible for them to get so busy with those activities that they pass on the "busyness" to their children without passing on the underlying motivations for those activities. We must take time with our children to share the reasons we are motivated to act, so they will understand the inner revival as well as participate in the outer reforms. If this is not done, the next generation will not continue the revival.

This principle has been apparent in most Christian movements. We are still caught up in the activities of the restoration movement, but largely without the zeal of our forefathers. Why? The practices have been passed on, but the reasons and motivations behind many of them have not. We have received their conclusions, but we do not know how or why they achieved them.

The same may be true in some congregations. The activities of the congregation may carry over into the next generation, but often the zeal and motivations are not there. Compromises and changes begin to occur.

The activities of a Bible college may continue for a hundred years, but do the administration and faculty share with the founders the reasons for the imperative existence of the college? The second generation is crucial in Christian education.

Or how about between the pulpit and the pew? The preacher may be extremely zealous for personal evangelism, or foreign missions, or benevolent work. The congregation follows suit and carries on the activities suggested by the emphasis of the preacher. But if the preacher does not share his reasons and motivations behind those activities, the activities will dwindle when he leaves.

What happens to cause such a cycle? We get so busy keeping up the externals that we neglect the responsibility of teaching. After all, teaching is less than spectacular. Progress in it cannot be measured as assuredly or as quickly as progress in other activities. Teaching requires great patience, for it takes a long time for ideas and motivations to take hold in peoples' minds.

The Hebrew children of their wandering parents obeyed, while their parents did not. The children brought revival to the nation. They got extremely busy winning battles on many fronts, but they neglected the weightier matter of teaching the motivations behind those battles. The next generation carried on those activities (Joshua 24:31). From the outside, there did not seem to be any difference between these two generations. But after a while a vast difference was discovered: "And all that generation also were gathered to their fathers; and there arose another generation after them who did not know the Lord, nor yet the work which He had done for Israel" (Judges 2:10).

What a tragedy! They inherited activities without attitudes, a movement without a motivation, practices without principles, a revival without a reason.

We today are reaping the results of an emphasis on practices and methods rather than on meaning and content. We are basically a Bible-ignorant people. We are having a tough time answering some of the grave issues of our day because we do not know what God would say about it and we do not know how to find out. Our young people and adults alike are hungry to know what the Bible says, but there are few who can teach them how to study it.

The revival of the Hebrews became empty because they did not know the motivations behind their many practices and they "did evil in the sight of the Lord, and served the Baals" (Judges 2:11). And they did not even see what was wrong with following another religion! They felt one was as good as another. They forsook the Lord (Judges 2:12, 13).

A Pitiful Sight

The book of Judges deals with 450 years of the Hebrew history, and what a pitiful picture it is! At the end of this period, the situation is no better than at the beginning, for we read, "Everyone did what was right in his own eyes" (Judges 21:25).

There were many periods of revival during those years, but they were shallow and selfish and did not last. Every revival was followed by a turning away from the Lord, acceptance of other gods, and enslavement to human conquerors. The Hebrews would then repent of their wrongs and cry out to God for help. God would answer by sending a deliverer. They would reform for a time, but the next generation would forsake God because the preceding one had not taught their children the reasons behind their actions. (The pattern is summarized in Judges 2:11-19.)

The deliverers (judges) are to be commended for bringing freedom to the people, but it seems that they failed to implement the teaching that would have given the next generation reasons to be loyal to God. The judges were too busy in activities. What they did was good, but they did not do enough.

Civil war eventually broke out among the Israelites (Judges 20:12-48), immorality increased as well as idol worship (Judges 2:11, 13; 8:27, 33; 10:6), priests hired themselves out to others (18:4), Levites took concubines (19:1), homosexuality as in the days of Sodom arose (19:22), and people did their own thing, independent of others (21:25).

But God's grace is greater than man's circumstances. In the blackest night God would respond to their pitiful cries for help. God used some leaders we probably would not. One of His judges was a woman (Judges 4). She was the civil, military, and religious leader of the entire nation. She was used by God as successfully as the male judges.

God sees potentiality in people that we often do not. Jephthah's mother was a prostitute, and he was illegitimate. Can you imagine how he felt filling out his work application forms—mother's occupation _____? He lived with his father, who was married to another woman. His brothers were sons of his father's wife, and eventually kicked him out. Jephthah joined a gang of worthless hoods who probably raided the "filling stations and drug stores" of their day. How could God use a roughneck ruffian like that? But God's Spirit came upon Jephthah, and he became one of God's faithful deliverers (Judges 11). He was listed alongside of Abraham, Moses, Gideon, Samson, and David in God's "Hall of Fame" (Hebrews 11:32).

Regardless of how bleak our circumstances may be—a nation like the inconsistent Hebrews or an individual who has hit bottom like Jephthah—God's grace is sufficient. But He needs people through whom His concern can be communicated to communities. His restoration movement will not advance where there are no people who will bring God's redemption and forgiveness to bear upon the consciousness of the people.

Along with the Jephthahs must work the Moseses—leaders who will rehearse what God has done in the past and who will instill within the minds of the people not just freedom with restoration, but faith with reasons. God teaches us in His use of Jephthah that He can and will use you and me if we are willing to bring God's grace and instruction into the very center of man's situations. But we must know in whom we believe, and why, if we intend to make a lasting contribution to our children and grandchildren. They deserve no less than that.

10

The Unchanging Message

Deuteronomy 26; Joshua 24

It has been observed that religious movements have often followed the same pattern. During a period of stress, a challenging *message* will stir men into a *movement*. A *machine* emerges to keep the movement alive, but eventually the machine becomes a *mortuary*. In the past few chapters, we have seen the Hebrews pass through the first three parts of the cycle, but they did not quite reach the mortuary stage (dead). Why not?

A religious movement does not have to follow that pattern. History is not a determined cycle that has to repeat itself. What happens at one stage of history influences the next stage, but the chain of events is not unalterable.

What prevented the Hebrews from entering the stage of the "grave" can also keep our Christianity alive. A leader who will not allow the passing of time or the changing environment to separate him from the heritage of his forefathers or from their challenging and unchanging message is needed. During and up to the end of that first generation, the Hebrews had Moses, who reechoed the message of Mount Sinai (Deuteronomy). During and up to the end of the second generation, they had Joshua, who reechoed the emphasis of his teacher, Moses, and thus the emphasis of the original message.

These men did not change the emphases of their messages to fit in with their changing times, and neither should we. It is a continual temptation to be so creative with the message of God that we change its content; when the content is changed, the challenge is changed. It becomes popular to say about a teaching of the Bible, "That does not apply to us either in principle or in practice." When that is believed, the mortuary stage is just ahead.

Of course we cannot impose all the practices of Jesus' day on ours. We do not carry baggage for Roman soldiers a second mile, and we do not greet others with a "holy kiss." Much of the teaching from Jesus and the apostles was poured into the culture of that day. But the principles and challenges are the same for a culture with interstate highways, fork lifts, jet planes, the Mayo clinic, and rockets to the moon.

The New Testament covenant can be shared and renewed in any culture. Some practices are to remain just exactly as they were in Jesus' day. Those that apply to the essentials of becoming a Christian are not tied to any particular culture. The gospel, the good news that unites a person with Christ, never changes. But some of the ways we apply our new life in Christ may vary from time to time and culture to culture. The principles behind those practices are, however, eternal and unchanging.

For example, the principle of caring for a brother in need can be fulfilled by using many different practices depending upon the culture and the situation. We may sew clothes for him, give him some of our goods, find him a job, give him money, or teach him how to provide for himself.

Important Messages

Moses and Joshua preached the same kind of message in order to keep God's covenant continuously before the people. Many aspects of their messages were parallel, even though they were given a generation apart:

(1) Each called for the people to remember what God had done in the past (Deuteronomy 1—3; Joshua 23:3-5; 24:2-13). That same approach was used in the New Testament. Peter was not ashamed to replow old ground:

> Therefore, I shall always be ready to remind you of these things, even though you already know them, and have been established in the truth which is present with you. And I consider it right, as long as I am in this earthly dwelling, to stir you up by way of reminder.
> —2 Peter 1:12, 13

This is an apostolic precedent that we had better follow. There is a need to hear the "old, old story" again and again, even though everyone in the congregation is a "regular." If we are always wanting to spin off something new, our children will be cut off from the familiar old story.

One of the problems with the people in Athens was that they were always wanting to hear something new (Acts 17:21). They would attend a meeting to hear something new, but not to be reminded of something old. Are we becoming like that?

Many people are saying that revival meetings are a thing of the past. No doubt they are not of use as evangelistic tools in some places, but perhaps we should not scrap them. Let us instead implement them to function as their name implies—*revival,* not evangelistic meetings. Why not use the week to remind the people of what God has done through Jesus? Perhaps the evangelistic emphasis has waned because many of the members are too remote from that old, old story.

Why should we remind the people? Peter says it this way: "And I will also be diligent that at any time after my departure you may be able to call these things to mind" (2 Peter 1:15). This is one imperative that will help keep our Christianity from becoming a mortuary.

(2) Moses and Joshua called the people to keep the word of God (Deuteronomy 4—27; Joshua 23:6; 24:14). They did not challenge the people to come to a spiritual smorgasbord to take or leave what they liked or did not like. "Be very firm, then, to keep and do *all* that is written . . ." (Joshua 23:6).

Jesus gave the apostles the same challenge: "Teaching them to observe *all* that I commanded you" (Matthew 28:20). We are not just to remind the people of what they already know. They would become secure and complacent; they would not reach on to maturity or be able to teach others (Hebrews 5:11— 6:3). Reminding must be coupled with teaching *all* that Jesus and the apostles taught. There are many gems of truth and practice in the New Testament that are not often shared or considered seriously, and we are the poorer for it.

We should not just keep emphasizing our favorite doctrine and stories. Such a practice maintains sectarianism. And if all we do in our Christian educational efforts is race through the Bible every six years, we are aiming toward the mortuary.

(3) Moses and Joshua warned the people against drowning in their environment (Deuteronomy 7:2; 13:1-3; Joshua 23:7-12). Spending time in remembrance and in teaching God's Word is a divine deterrent to following our environment wherever it leads us. The church cannot hide from the world. We are to be " a city set on a hill" (Matthew 5:14), to be light, salt, and leaven. We can only do that by staying in the world. Jesus mentioned this fact

in His prayer: "I do not ask Thee to take them out of the world, but to keep them from the evil one" (John 17:15).

When Paul warned the Corinthians not to associate with the immoral, they misunderstood him to mean to isolate themselves. Paul corrected that notion: "I did not at all mean with the immoral people of this world, or with the covetous and swindlers, or with idolaters; for then you would have to go out of the world. But actually I wrote to you not to associate with any so-called brother if he should be an immoral person . . ." (1 Corinthians 5:10, 11). But then the Corinthians went too far: they not only associated with the immoral, but began to participate in some of their practices. So Paul had to correct them again in 2 Corinthians 6:14—7:1. He told them to isolate themselves from non-Christian practices (but not non-Christian people).

In recent years, the line between the practices of Christains and those of non-Christians has not been clearly drawn. People can come into the church with little or no alteration in life-styles or habits. It has been said of Joe Christian, "We like Joe; he's just like one of the boys. He laughs at our dirty jokes and drinks just like the rest of us." This blurring of the difference is one route to the mortuary. Christians are to be holy as God is holy; we must grow up to the stature of the Emmanuel, not the environment (1 Peter 1:15, 16; Ephesians 4:13-15; Colossians 2:6).

(4) Moses and Joshua spoke clearly about the wrath of God (Deuteronomy 28, 29; Joshua 24:19, 20). Neither did Jesus sweep the wrath of God under the rug. It is clear by His words that it will be difficult for some to enter God's kingdom (Luke 18:25), and that some will be cast into Hell (Matthew 25:41).

The apostles did not whitewash God's wrath or try to say just "nice" things. Even though it was not popular, Paul said, "For the wrath of God is revealed from heaven against all ungodliness and unrighteousness of men, who suppress the truth in unrighteousness (Romans 1:18). He was not "tickling their ears" when he said this:

> Do not be deceived; neither fornicators, nor idolaters, nor adulterers, nor effeminate, nor homosexuals, nor thieves, nor covetous, nor drunkards, nor revilers, nor swindlers, shall inherit the kingdom of God.
>
> —1 Corinthians 6:9, 10

Evidently Paul had never read *How to Win Friends and Influence People* or *The Power of Positive Thinking,* for he said that God

> will render to every man according to his deeds . . . to those who are selfishly ambitious and do not obey the truth, but obey unrighteousness, wrath and indignation. There will be tribulation and distress for every soul of man who does evil . . .   —Romans 2:6-9

Is it becoming unpopular to call sin "sin" and Hell "Hell"? If so, then we had better be unpopular. We are to call people to renewal. We must stand as blockades between the "machinery" and the "mortuary." We are to challenge our environment, not to be silenced by it.

(5) Moses and Joshua challenged their hearers to recommitment (Deuteronomy 10:12; 18:13; Joshua 24:14, 15, 22, 23). Recommitment involved three challenges: Respect God and serve Him in sincerity and in truth; make God Lord of your life; and choose today whom you will serve—the gods of your environment or the God of the universe (Joshua 24:14, 15). One or the other had to go; the people could not follow both.

Jesus made this same challenge: "No one can serve two masters" (Matthew 6:24). The people had to decide what would be the guiding force in their lives.

You and I have that same need today. What are we living for? When we are faced with choices, what consistent principle do we really use to decide? If we decide on the side of God, is it by accident or by intent?

A Choice to Make

The renewing of people's commitment to God's covenant has always been accompanied by the preaching of leaders who include all these truths that Moses and Joshua included. But preaching is not all that is needed. The people must take the wax out of their ears, take off the casts that keep their necks from turning, and hear, heed, and turn to the Lord of the universe.

The generation to which Moses spoke heeded his words and entered the promised land. They did not take their religion to the mortuary. The generation to which Joshua spoke did well on the surface, but they did not follow *all* God commanded. They did not take seriously God's command, "These words . . . you shall teach . . . to your sons" (Deuteronomy 6:6, 7). They got so caught up in the machinery that their children "did not know the Lord, nor yet the work which He had done for Israel" (Judges 2:10).

Yet the Hebrews made their choice and committed themselves to serve the Lord. We must be careful about making such commitments, for God takes them seriously. He will hold us accountable and make us witnesses to our words. He will expect our future practices to coincide with our stated purpose. Despite the good intentions of the Hebrews, the stage of the mortuary was getting closer.

But the pattern of this religious movement will be interrupted by other human blockades. Are we of the church moving into the mortuary stage with our Christianity? Or are we serving as human blockades with God's message? God intends us to be just that.

11

Gideon: God's Courageous Man

Judges 6—8

In Hiding

God's people were in a mess again. This time they re-treated. With the enemy active all around them, they took the "low visibility" approach by hiding in dens and caves (Judges 6:2). After all, isn't crawling into our shells so we can't be seen or heard a pretty good self-protection? The Hebrews thought so then, and many of God's people seem to think so today.

Our "dens and caves" come in various shapes and sizes—from formal monasteries to informal cliques. They are anything that keeps us from challenging the oppo-nents to God's way.

While the Hebrews stayed in their secure hiding places, their enemies destroyed their sustenance (Judges 6:4). The same can happen to us if we bury our heads in the sand, do not see what is going on around us, and do not evaluate the implications. While we nestle in security, it is possible that some of the principles and practices upon which we have stood have been destroyed by anti-Christian termites. How sad! We didn't even detect a problem until too much was eaten away.

Christian colleges that once were fundamental have turned into strongholds of liberalism; music, art, and literature have become eroded—while God's people have remained in their "dens and caves." The enemy grows as locusts with devastation in their paths (Judges 6:4, 5).

But throughout history, God has always had courageous people who were challenged to activity by the threatening situation. His "Hall of Fame" lists many (Hebrews 11). One of them was Gideon.

The Leader, Gideon

Gideon was no "giant of a man" when God called him. He even questioned that God could be with him: "My lord, if the Lord is with us, why then has all this happened to us" (Judges 6:12, 13). When things haven't gone so well, aren't we also prone to blame God?

The people had gotten into many messes because of their unfaithfulness, not because of God's (Judges 6:8-10). He was always there to deliver them. God called Gideon to be courageous in faithfulness, which is the qualification that has historically made people function for God—and made them famous. None of God's leaders were famous before they were courageous. And they were not courageous because they knew what the outcome of their actions would be. They were not sure what God had in store for them, but they did as God asked.

At times we think that we have to be a "somebody" to be used significantly by God. Hebrew history certainly does not uphold that theory. Even Jesus emptied himself of His divine form to undertake humble service, which in turn led to His exaltation (Philippians 2:5-11).

God's people were in a bind. They were hemmed in by the enemy, and it looked like they might not survive. What could Gideon do? After all, he was just a farmer (Judges 6:11) who had no formal education in a Bible college, seminary, law school, or military academy. Shouldn't he just mind his own business? Yes, that was what he should do, because the welfare of God's people was his business.

But he saw himself as a "nobody"; "O Lord, how shall I deliver Israel? Behold, my family is the least . . . and I am the youngest" (Judges 6:15). God spoke to him, but he still did not believe that he could do anything significant. He asked for a sign from God (Judges 6:16-21). Many Christians today ask for signs in much the same way without realizing that to do so is a mark of disbelief rather than belief. If God's Word tells us our responsibility, as it did to Gideon, then we should obey without questioning. Gideon should be commended for following God, but his weakness of character in asking for a sign is not a good example for us.

Gideon's Commission

Gideon faced a big task—to stand against the false religions of his day (Judges 6:25). God is opposed to false religions, and so must God's people be. One of the first messages God gave to His people was, "I, the Lord your God, am a jealous God" (Exodus 20:5).

Jealousy can be good or bad. It is bad when motivated by self-gratification; it is good when it has the good of another person in mind. For instance, Bill is jealous because Barbara is going with Jim. But why? Does he know that Jim is no good for Barbara? And is his concern for Barbara for her own good? That is the requirement for godly jealousy (2 Corinthians 11:2). Or is it because Jim has Barbara's companionship when Bill wants it? This is jealousy with oneself in mind.

God is a jealous God. He is against false religions because He knows what harm they do to people. His zeal for people's good is the basis of His jealousy. Shouldn't we share that attitude of God? Are we really convinced that Christianity and only Christianity is the truth? Or do we go along with the philosophy of comparative religions and feel that one religion is as good as any other? Are we afraid to upset someone's culture with the message of Christ? Christ is the *only* way to salvation and freedom, and we had better start believing it.

But just being opposed to other religions is not enough. We must also replace the false religions with the true religion. That was the second part of God's commission to Gideon (Judges 6:26). Gideon was scared (6:27); he was not taking a popular stand (6:29, 30).

He would probably not be popular if he were alive and in our churches today either. It is not popular to say that people of other lands and other religions are condemned even if they do not ever hear about God and Jesus. We hear it said, "As long as they do not know about Christ, their religion will not hurt them because of God's grace." How wrong we are! The totality of the Bible speaks against that statement.

Although Gideon's opposition was tough, he had support from a very important quarter—his own home. His father stood up for what he was doing (Judges 6:29-32). Is it possible that this support he got from home became the major reason Gideon progressed in being God's man? Do you support your children when they decide to get involved in God's way? When they write papers at school challenging the liberal thinking of our day, do you tend to tone them down so they will receive better grades? What is your reaction if they decide to go to Bible college instead of taking a scholarship to a state university?

It was not easy for Gideon, even though his family was behind him. He began to doubt, and he put out the fleece to test God. But once was not enough. Aren't we like that sometimes? Haven't you ever flipped a coin to determine God's will, and then when it did not turn out as you wanted, you flipped it again to make it two times out of three? Yes, Gideon was immature, but he was growing.

How are we supposed to make decisions today if we are not to "put out the fleece," flip a coin, call Jeanne Dixon, or "get the right feeling"? We are to use our minds to know God's *revealed* will for everyone (His universal will). There is no flexibility in that. But when we know that *revealed* will, we are left with many alternatives, the choices of which God has not revealed (whom to marry, where to live, etc.)

To make these decisions, we must use our minds to consider whether or not God's characteristics are the motivations for the choices we make, whether or not the choice fits in with our abilities and talents, squares with counsel from mature leaders, conforms to Biblical principles, and is within the realm of common sense.

God is in the guiding business, but He does not like to guide with the use of the "fleece." God prefers that we act out of faith and obedience on the basis of what we *know* to be His will (found in His Word). He has said,

> I will instruct you and teach you the way you should go; I will counsel you with my eye upon you. Be not like a horse or a mule, without understanding, which must be curbed with bit and bridle . . .
> —Psalm 32:8, 9, Revised Standard Version

God does not want us to be like mules who have to be "told" every turn to take. We are made in God's image; we are not mules. (For a more detailed discussion, see *How to Know the Will of God,* Standard Publishing, Order No. 40027).

Courageous Faithfulness

God's working with Gideon teaches us that God can do

great things through little people, and that the salvation of God's people does not depend upon big programs. God decreased Gideon's troops from many, many thousands to three hundred men (Judges 7:3-6). God did not want the people to think that success in their conquest was due to their great number and might (Judges 7:2).

How many times do small congregations rationalize how little they are doing because of their small size? Size is not the issue. Courageous faithfulness makes the difference. A courageous, committed minority is always more effective than a cowardly and uncommitted majority.

Jesus permitted the rich young ruler to walk away. He also watched many of His disciples leave Him (John 6:66). He saw His followers dwindle from thousands to 120 (John 6:10 to Acts 1:15). But He was not dismayed, because He knew that 120 followers with twelve courageous leaders would do more in spiritual warfare than five thousand men (plus women and children) who were in the battle just for what they could get out of it for themselves.

Gideon became great because he recognized his smallness and depended upon God's bigness. He did not build himself up. When some people complained because he did not use them in his spectacular activities (Judges 8:1), he replied that what they were doing was more important than what he was doing: "What have I done now in comparison with you? Is not the gleaning of the grapes of Ephraim better than the vintage of Abiezer?" (8:2). Gideon knew what all of us must come to realize and practice: in God's family, everybody is a somebody.

12

Strength
Out of Control

Judges 13—16

Samson, the Man

On the surface, it appeared that Samson had everything going for him. His beginning was the opposite of Jephthah's (Judges 11). He had parents dedicated to God; he had the Nazirite vow to become a "life recruit"; he had God-given abilities. He was able to be stirred by God and was not lazy.

All of these qualities were not enough to make him the kind of leader God's people needed. A life recruit who has lots of energy and ability can be useful if his emotions are channeled and directed, and if he has the right goals in mind. But he can be a hindrance if his character and goal-orientation are off base.

The moment a person becomes a Christian, he becomes a "life recruit," living his life under the lordship of

Jesus. Every person has God-given abilities, but those abilities are to be used unselfishly for the good of others, not self. Peter stated it this way: "As each one has received a special gift, employ it in serving one another, as good stewards of the manifold grace of God" (1 Peter 4:10). We present ourselves as living sacrifices to God as we use our differing gifts for others (Romans 12).

But without proper motives and priorities, it is possible to use our gifts selfishly. A person with the gift of leadership could head the Mafia. A person with the gift of teaching could use it to manipulate people to become followers of himself. Godlike character is needed to make proper use of God's *charisma* (grace-gift, abilities) to us.

Paul listed many of the abilities persons can have; then he exhorted his readers to use them with love and devotion for one another (1 Corinthians 13). He cautioned them against being haughty and repaying evil for evil (Romans 12:9-21).

When we first get a glimpse of Samson as a man, we can see the weakness of his character. He evidently had not been disciplined by his parents. He told his father what he wanted and expected to get it: "I saw a woman in Timnah, one of the daughters of the Philistines; now therefore, get her for me as a wife" (Judges 14:2). Here was a man who had vowed to follow God, and yet he was planning to marry a woman who had nothing in common with God or God's people. She would not be able to share in a godly purpose or methods. The two could not be yoked together as teammates.

Samson's parents knew that, and tried to persuade Samson not to marry her. But he was bent on having things his own way. He did not care about the advice of his parents or what God had to say about the matter (Joshua 23:11-13). Instead of honoring his parents, he demanded obedience from them. He was the only child of their old age and evidently was used to taking advantage of their devotion. After they advised him, he said,

"Get her for me, for she looks good to me" (Judges 14:3). Samson's philosophy of life seemed to be "I want what I want when I want it." No wonder he was the first judge who was not able to deliver Israel from her enemy. He simply began the deliverance (Judges 13:5), and it was a meager beginning.

I wonder if Samson thought, "I can change my wife after we are married. She will see things my way." Many, many potential leaders and workers in God's vineyard have been sidetracked because they married mates who did not share their purpose in life. Such marriages have taken their toll in every area of service—Sunday-school teachers, youth sponsors, elders, deacons, choir members, callers, benevolent workers, preachers, evangelists, missionaries, college teachers, etc.

Samson's character breakdown, I believe, began with his parents. They did not teach him how to handle his emotions or to be a serving, submitting person. They probably thought he would not respect them or talk to them freely if they disciplined him. But that theory backfired. Without discipline as a boy, he did not respect them when he became a man. He lived one of the most undisciplined lives we read about in the Bible.

We as Christian parents must learn from this example. Our Christian struggle against opposition must not cause us to bypass disciplining our children. They will be tomorrow's leaders. How they lead will be partly determined by how they are being led in the home. It is not enough that we are dedicated, or that we have discovered our children's abilities and nurtured them, or even that they have dedicated themselves to God. They must be taught self-control and helped to develop the proper priorities.

Samson had kept up one external sign of keeping his vow to God—his hair was uncut. Sometimes in our churches when we are selecting leaders, we look for dedication only through external and measurable signs (college degrees, regular attendance, Christian parents, hair that *is* cut!) We need to be more concerned with a person's sincerity, humility, and serving attitude.

The record does not show much of these gentler attributes in Samson. He was arrogant with his parents as well as with his enemies. Other judges enlisted the repentant people in the battle against their oppressors, but Samson was a single-handed fighter, a one-man army. David was a great warrior who gave God the credit for his victories. See Psalm 124, for example. But Samson's psalm spoke only of what Samson had done (Judges 15:16). The Spirit of the Lord came upon him with such tremendous power that he could tear a lion apart with his bare hands or beat an army with a bit of bone (Judges 14:5, 6; 15:14, 15); but the normal fruit of God's Spirit includes patience, kindness, gentleness, and self-control (Galatians 5:22, 23), and we do not see much of these in the record of Samson's life.

Along with the magnificent strength of the man, we have to note his pitiful weakness. Invincible as he was with men, he was a pushover with women. They could wrap him around their little fingers, and they did (Judges 14:16, 17). Still he was reckless in his affairs with them. Such affairs brought him into danger repeatedly, and finally led to his downfall (Judges 16:1-21).

God can use people in spite of their weaknesses and follies. If He could not, there would be no one on earth that He could use. He chose Samson to begin delivering the people of Israel from the Philistines, and Samson did that. It seems plain that he could have done more and continued longer if he had been more fully devoted to God and the mission God gave him, but what he accomplished is still amazing. His character was probably better than we may suppose from a quick glance at the record. Ferocious as he was to the enemy, he did not turn against his own people even when they turned against him (Judges 15:9-15). Though he sang only of himself when he was victorious, he did call on God in emergencies (Judges 15:18, 19; 16:27-30). He judged Israel for twenty years (Judges 15:20), and may have done much good that is not recorded. We do know that his faith in God was such that he did great things and had a place among the faithful who are named in the eleventh chapter of Hebrews.

Application for Us

We can learn from this story of a man who was gifted with special strength from God, but who failed to make full use of the possibilities before him. It can be dangerous for us to discover our God-given abilities, for they can be used to help others or to get gain for ourselves. Our abilities are like Samson's in one way at least: they are God's gift to us. Do we make full use of them in serving God and helping His people? Or do we keep up the externals of our faith (attendance, giving, etc.) and seek to influence people just to feed our own egos and to hear people say what fine Christians we are?

We must avoid this latter approach as we struggle against the spiritual opponents of our day. To be at our best in the struggle, we must take seriously the qualifications of our leaders that God outlined to Timothy and Titus. Samson did not show many of these qualities. God wants a man who is the husband of one wife (women cannot be his weakness); he is to be temperate, gentle, not quick-tempered. But with all his gentleness he is to manage his own household, not to be a pushover to his wife's every whim. He is not to be self-willed, living for himself.

God revealed these leadership qualities because they will stand the test of opposition and responsibility. The opposite character traits, even when accompanied by great abilities, do not make a man effective in any lasting way in opposing the enemies of God or in replacing them with the friends of God.

Samson's life ended on a pitiful but triumphant note. He was blind and bound in the house of the Philistines— the very people from whom he was supposed to deliver the Hebrews. Perhaps more poignantly than ever before, he recognized his dependency upon God (Judges 16:28). God honored that recognition and gave him a final victory in his death.

It seems clear that there was no notable national repentance under Samson's leadership as there had been under other judges. We do not see a fervent desire on the part of the people for deliverance from the Philistines who had oppressed them for forty years (Judges 13:1). Samson could not even find three hundred faithful men, as Gideon had done. His personal victories may have made a contribution to Israel's later victory over their oppressors (1 Samuel 7); but Samson only began a deliverance, while each of the other judges completed a deliverance.

An undisciplined leader can slow down the struggle for victory and freedom. Samson was a model to show the Hebrew people what potential strength was available to them with God. But he was a model who also showed that weakness can corrode that strength if full devotion to God is lacking. May we learn from the model of Samson. May we make full use of the abilities God gives us, and not fetter them with selfish follies.

13

The Use or Abuse of Liberty

Judges 21:25; 1 Samuel 7—10

True Freedom

The struggle for freedom had been both long and difficult for the Israelites. God's freedom does not automatically bring physical serenity, but often continual struggling. Being free in God does not automatically mean we are mature. We are unshackled to become all that God can enable us to become; whether we do so depends upon how we use the liberty we have been given. There is no way to be free from responsiblity. More freedom brings more responsibility.

God's freedom is not just loosing us from the tyranny of things; it is allowing us to be responsible servants to others. Only as we unselfishly spend our thoughts, energies, talents, and trust in caring for others have we functionally entered true freedom. Jesus had that kind of freedom and is our example. He was free from the tyranny of Satan, from His environment, from things, from pressure groups, and from His own selfishness.

At the same time Jesus was a submitted person. He was submitted to live in accordance with God's kind of freedom—not to be enslaved to living for self. He lived not to please himself, but for the good of others (Romans 15:2, 3).

It is only as we turn from self to God and to others that we find ourselves becoming fully human—in the image of God. Liberty in God is living in accordance with our created nature as children of an unselfish and good God. (See "How to Live in True Freedom" in *The Gospel According to Paul,* Standard Publishing, order No. 2280).

A New King

We can abuse our liberty by viewing freedom and the goodness of God as license to do "our own thing." If we decide to turn away from God, we will turn away from others, even those in our own "group," and finally from ourselves. We will start looking for another "king" over our lives.

This is the path the Israelites took. They had been freed from the enslavement of Egypt for several generations, but they had hardly crawled outside their own selfish interests. From the third day after they were given freedom, their pilgrimage was filled with grumblings against God every time they did not get their way. They abused their liberty. Except for brief periods of revival, they continued to worship pagan gods.

The people of God were standing on the brink of changing their government from a theocracy (rule of God) to a monarchy (rule of one person). On the surface, it is difficult to blame them, for some of their leaders were shoddy representatives of God's way of governing (1 Samuel 8:1-3). The elders liked what they saw in outside nations better than what they saw on the inside of their own nation, so they asked for a king (1 Samuel 8:5).

It is a sad state of affairs when leaders within the community of God are not as moral as leaders outside His community, but it is even sadder when God's people openly vote to become just like those who are not of God. They thought they would be safer with a king than under God's care (1 Samuel 8:20).

Is it possible that they wanted to be like the other nations because the other nations did not have to listen to God and they seemed to be faring pretty well? After all, it would be easier for each generation to listen to and obey its king than to keep rehearsing what God had done, to teach their children His way, and to accept guilt when things did not go well. When people listen to and follow a king, he can get all the blame when things go wrong. So the Israelites turned from studying God's way and handed the business over to the king. Under the kings, God's Word was so sidetracked that years after the king system took over, God's Word was accidently found— *stored away* (2 Kings 22).

I wonder if we ever follow that procedure. Christians are a nation within a nation. Paul advises, "Let every person be in subjection to the governing authorities" (Romans 13:1). It is possible to misuse that advice, imagining that it releases us from our responsibility to God's Word. Why study the Bible? We can just obey the President and Congress. If our responsibility begins and ends there, a lot of inspiration and energy were wasted in the writing of the rest of the New Testament. Americanism is not equated with Christianity, and we had better admit it. The best thing we can do for our nation is to Christianize it by preaching and following Jesus Christ. The worst thing we can do is to Americanize our Christianity so that the Christian community marches to the same drum as the non-Christian community. We are lost if we lose our distinctive character.

The Hebrews wanted to become like others, and they

did. If we do not take seriously what history has to teach us (1 Corinthians 10:6), we will probably repeat it. And God allows it to happen. God will give us up to our desires whenever we are determined to follow them (Romans 1:18-32). He allowed the Israelites to have a king, but He did not approve of it. "I gave you a king in My anger" (Hosea 13:11).

When the Hebrews called for a king, God made it clear that they were rejecting Him as their king (1 Samuel 8:7, 8). It did not have to be a rejection of Him. A monarchy could work, but only if the people and the king lived under God's will and way. A monarchy could be a theocracy as well, but only if the king's king was God. This is what God meant when He said through Samuel:

> Now therefore, here is the king whom you have chosen. . . . If you will fear the Lord and serve Him, and listen to His voice and not rebel against the command of the Lord, then both you and also the king who reigns over you will follow the Lord your God.   —1 Samuel 12:13, 14

No human government can release God's people from obedience to God. Peter said, "We must obey God rather than men" (Acts 5:29). Paul said that God is the "only Sovereign, the King of kings and Lord of lords" (1 Timothy 6:15). Our duty to Him is above all our other duties.

The Hebrews were given the responsibility for making the monarchy work. It would work if both the king and the people would follow God. The responsibility for its failure to work also rested upon the people: "And if you will not listen to the voice of the Lord, but rebel against the command of the Lord, then the hand of the Lord will be against you" (1 Samuel 12:15).

God knew the potential danger of a human king ruling over God's people. He knew that when the king ceased to live under God, the monarchy would turn into a *man*-archy. God warned them,

> This will be the procedure of the king who will reign over
> you: he will take your sons and place them for himself in
> his chariots and among his horsemen and they will run
> before his chariots. And he will appoint for himself com-
> manders of thousands and of fifties, and some to do his
> plowing and to reap his harvest and to make his weapons
> of war and equipment for his chariots. He will also take
> your daughters for perfumers and cooks and bakers. And
> he will take the best of your fields and your vineyards and
> your olive groves, and give them to his servants. And he
> will take a tenth of your seed and of your vineyards, and
> give to his officers and to his servants—1 Samuel 8:11-16.

Such happenings could be avoided if the people and the king lived under God. But they came to pass because the people ignored God. They tried to please the king instead of God. And they pleased him with wickedness instead of righteousness (Hosea 7:3).

The shift is seen in the change in the role of the Holy Spirit. Up to this time, the Holy Spirit had directed the good leaders of Israel. He directed the first three kings as long as they were willing to follow His leading. Most of the later kings were not open to being led by God, and the people were not willing to be led by men who fol- lowed God's leading (the prophets).

As the activity of the Spirit among the kings lessened because of their selfish interests, the activity of the Spirit among the prophets quickened. The prophets were in- spired men calling the people to obedience to God. But the people did not listen. Who wants to see and hear a preacher instead of a king? No one, especially when he forgets that it was by a prophet that God brought Israel out of Egypt (Hosea 12:13).

Yes, the struggle for freedom is tough. With slavery of all forms around us, it is easy to be lured by what seems most appealing for the now generation—another kind of slavery. The temptation to adopt what seems to work in the world around us, even if it does not square with God's

Word, will always dangle in front of God's people. One of Satan's well-thought-out intentions is to slowly assimilate us into the surrounding environment. He would like for us to move from low visibility to invisibility.

We can slip into Satan's pitfalls even with the best of intentions. The temptation to do what others are doing because it works well comes in many forms, depending upon the times. The more effectively it works, the less we feel a need to study God's Word and share it with others, for we think we have "found the secret."

Right now some churches are facing the temptation to shift from management by a number of elders to a pastor system in which the pastor is *the* authority in the church. It seems to be working for many growing congregations. One-man management makes businesses grow; it keeps the Mafia alive. But we must consider Jesus' words, "The rulers of the Gentiles lord it over them. . . . It is not so among you, but whoever wishes to become great among you shall be your servant" (Matthew 20:25, 26).

A Positive Outlook

Let us not have a defeatist attitude; let us have a dedicated attitude. Let us remember that God's grace is bigger than man's circumstances. The history of the Israelites is not pretty, but God's faithfulness to them is. God continued to be a part of their history. He continued to care. His love is splattered all over the Old Testament history, and that same love is available to us.

Amid our human weakness stands God's strength, eager to become a part of our lives. Amid our slaveries stands His freedom that comes in the person of Jesus Christ: "If therefore the Son shall make you free, you shall be free indeed" (John 8:36).

Years after the history we have considered in this book, the still-fettered Israelites asked what they should do to have freedom. Peter answered, "Repent, and let each of you be baptized in the name of Jesus Christ for the forgiveness of your sins; and you shall receive the gift of the Holy Spirit" (Acts 2:38). "Where the Spirit of the Lord is, there is liberty" (2 Corinthians 3:17). The Jews of that day needed liberty from legalism and freedom from the fetters of their fathers' hard hearts (Acts 7:51). Only in Jesus can we have the redemption that sets us free (Hebrews 9:12, Galatians 3:13, Romans 3:24). God's relationship with the Israelites in the Old Testament was to lead them to Jesus (Galatians 3:24). Faith frees from fetters. Let us experience our exodus from slavery through Jesus our deliverer. And then let us walk in His true freedom (Romans 6). The Israelites could only walk *toward* that freedom, but we can walk *in* it. The struggle for freedom has ended. The life in liberty has begun in Jesus. So let us live.